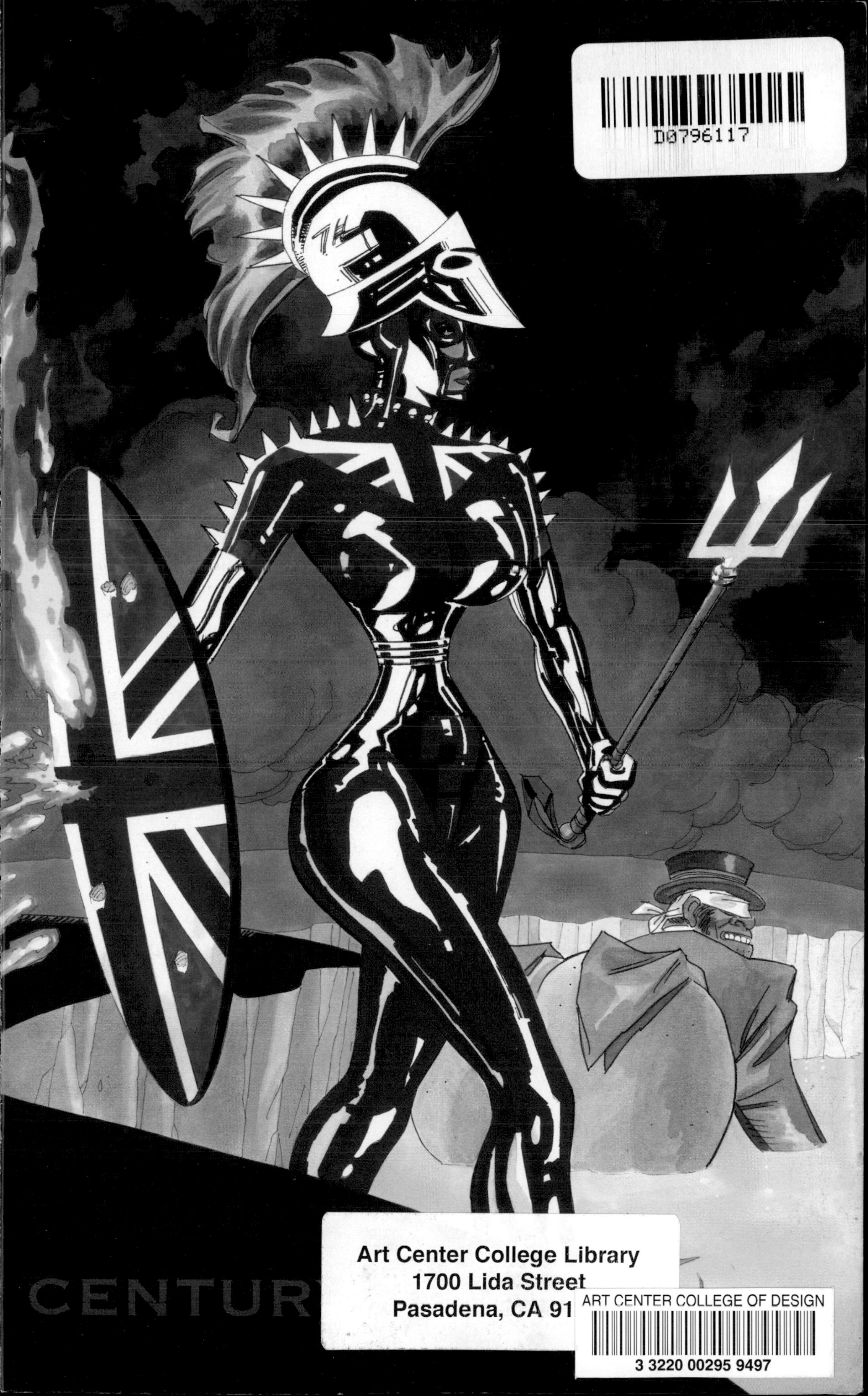
CENTUR

KREDITKRUNCH

What is KreditKrunch? The world's smallest platform for funding dubious pictorialisations. Help our creators produce another project. Give generously! **Learn more!**

The League of Extraordinary Gentleme

A Comics project both here and across the pond by Al, Kev, Ben and Todd • make a statement

THIS ENDEAVOR WILL ONLY BE FUNDED IF AT LEAST £5000 IS PLEDGED AT SOME POINT BEFORE WE'RE FINISHED. WE'RE COMPLETELY AT YOUR MERCY, YOU DEVILS.

BACK THIS PROJECT £5 minimum

3 BACKERS | **£15** PLEDGED | **LOTS** OF DAYS TO GO

PLEDGE £200 OR MORE — 0 BACKERS

Writer seeks funds for Osman spare parts for enlightenment and astral travel. Prepared to divulge information from December 21st 2012 of considerable interest to people with Christmas plans! Contact via ether or: alanmoore@home.tom

PLEDGE £100 OR MORE — 0 BACKERS

Artist of doubtful taste will undertake female portraits. No subject too large. Contact: kevinoneill@whatsitmeanttobe.tom

PLEDGE £50 OR MORE — 0 BACKERS

Complimentary colour therapist with own mood wheel will retint your mojo. Contact: bigbendimagmaliw@tokyofop.tom

PLEDGE £5 OR MORE

3 BACKERS

Reed and rite calligraphy and design course now booking. Contact: professortoddklei @comixink.tom

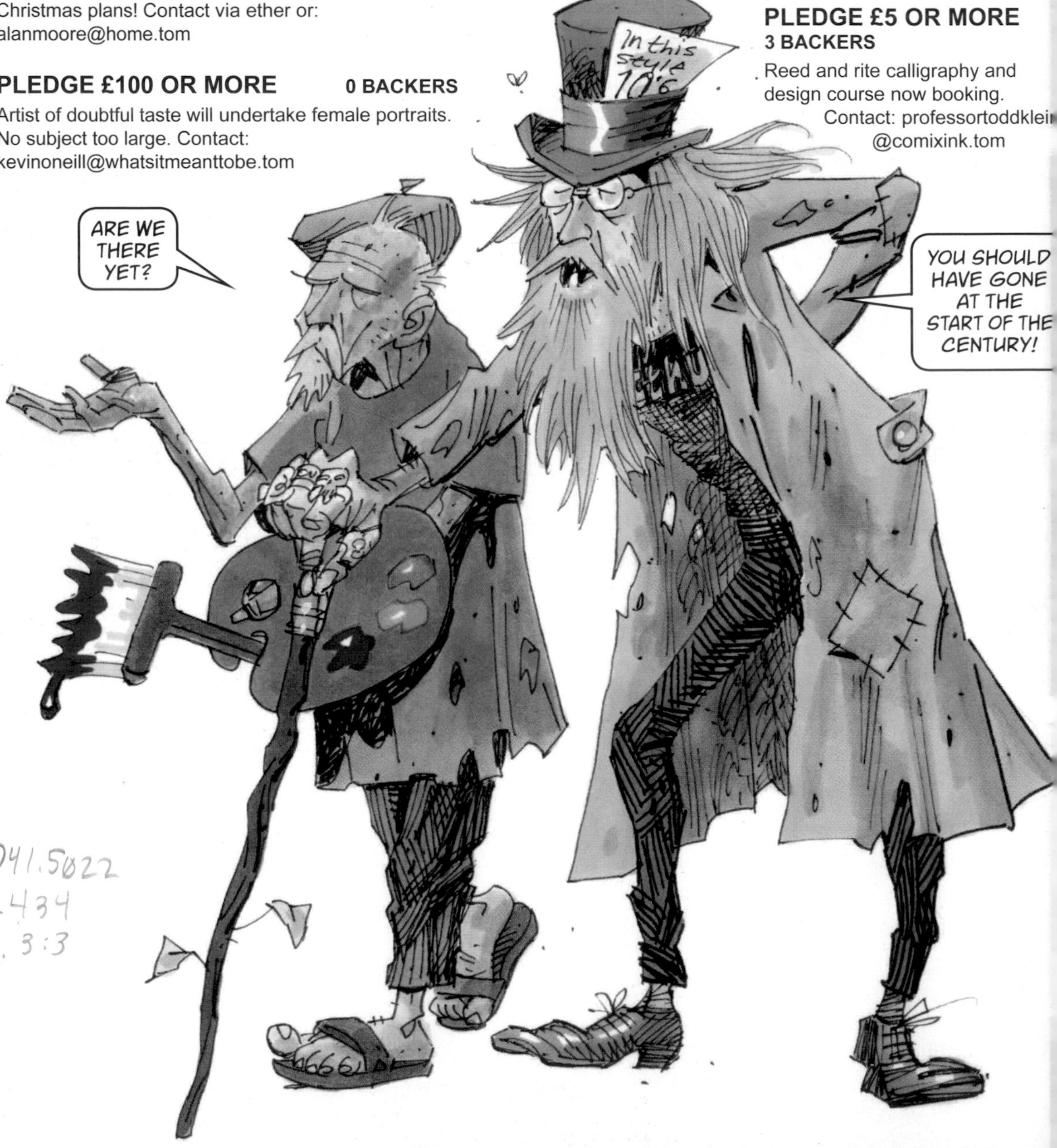
In this style 10/6
ARE WE THERE YET?
YOU SHOULD HAVE GONE AT THE START OF THE CENTURY!

The editor of this book is **Chris Staros.** It's co-published by **TOP SHELF PRODUCTIONS, Chris Staros & Brett Warnoc** publishers, and **KNOCKABOUT COMICS, Tony Bennett & Josh Palmano,** publishers. Special thanks to **Iain Sinclair, Michael Moorcock** and **Armando Iannucci.** Visit our online catalogues at www.topshelfcomix.com and www.knockabout com. **Have a question?** Ask the editor directly. Go ahead, ask. See what joy it brings you.

ASK A QUESTION

WELL, I NEVER.

YOU'RE CORPORAL ORLANDO, THEN? THE HERO OF THE HOUR, OR SO THEY TELL ME.

MIND IF I SIT DOWN?

AND WHO THE FUCK ARE YOU...

...SIR?

HA. I'M COLONEL CUCKOO.

I'M A... A *COMBAT* VETERAN. A BIT LIKE YOURSELF, IF I'M RIGHT.

NAPOLEONIC WARS, I STARTED OUT. WHAT ABOUT YOU?

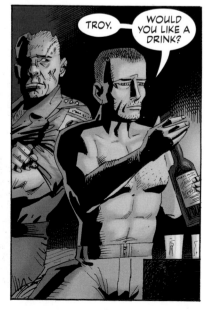

TROY.

WOULD YOU LIKE A DRINK?

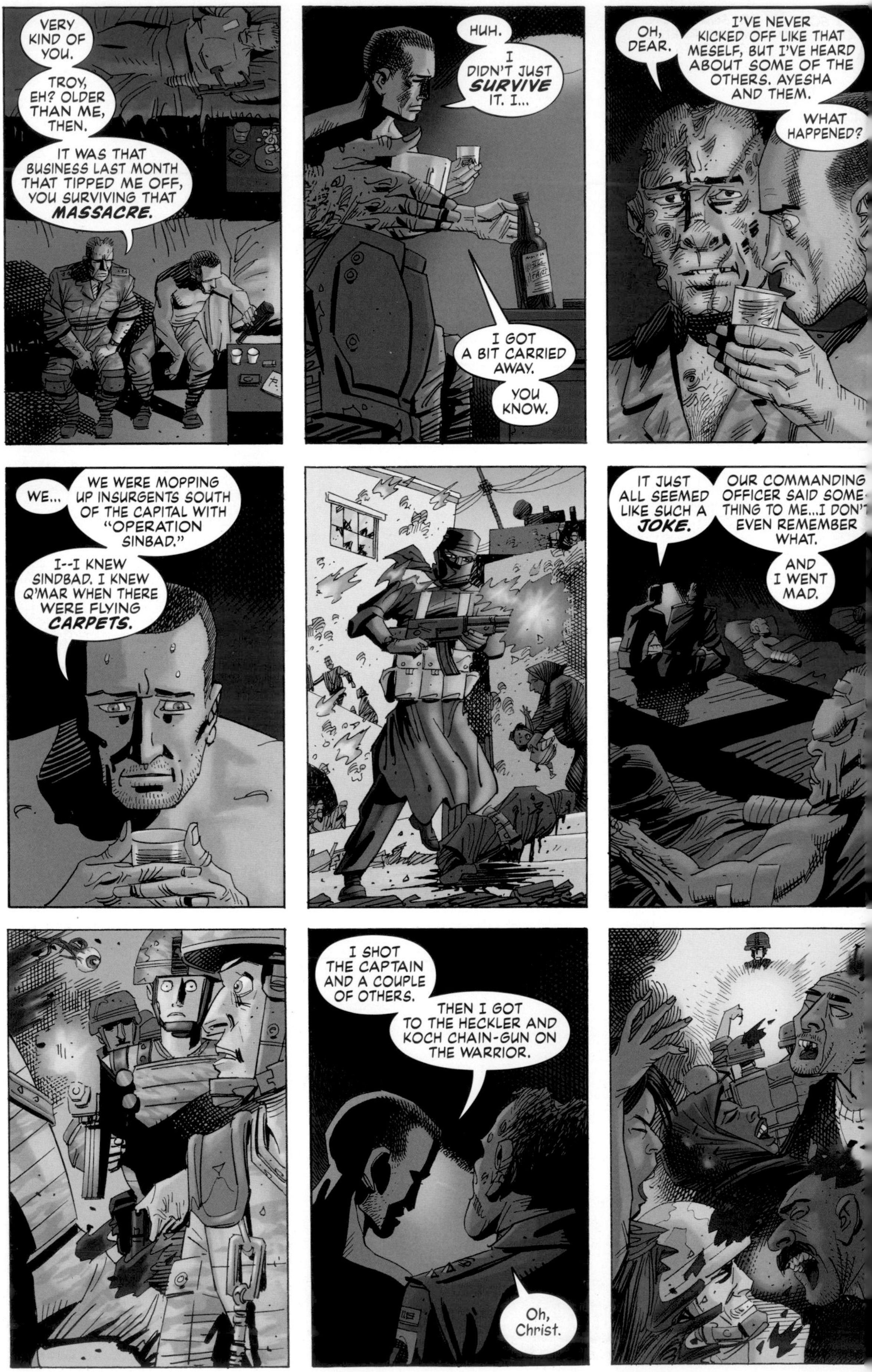
VERY KIND OF YOU.
TROY, EH? OLDER THAN ME, THEN.
IT WAS THAT BUSINESS LAST MONTH THAT TIPPED ME OFF, YOU SURVIVING THAT MASSACRE.
HUH.
I DIDN'T JUST SURVIVE IT. I...
I GOT A BIT CARRIED AWAY.
YOU KNOW.
OH, DEAR.
I'VE NEVER KICKED OFF LIKE THAT MESELF, BUT I'VE HEARD ABOUT SOME OF THE OTHERS. AYESHA AND THEM.
WHAT HAPPENED?
WE...
WE WERE MOPPING UP INSURGENTS SOUTH OF THE CAPITAL WITH "OPERATION SINBAD."
I--I KNEW SINDBAD. I KNEW Q'MAR WHEN THERE WERE FLYING CARPETS.
IT JUST ALL SEEMED LIKE SUCH A JOKE.
OUR COMMANDING OFFICER SAID SOMETHING TO ME...I DON'T EVEN REMEMBER WHAT.
AND I WENT MAD.
I SHOT THE CAPTAIN AND A COUPLE OF OTHERS.
THEN I GOT TO THE HECKLER AND KOCH CHAIN-GUN ON THE WARRIOR.
Oh, Christ.

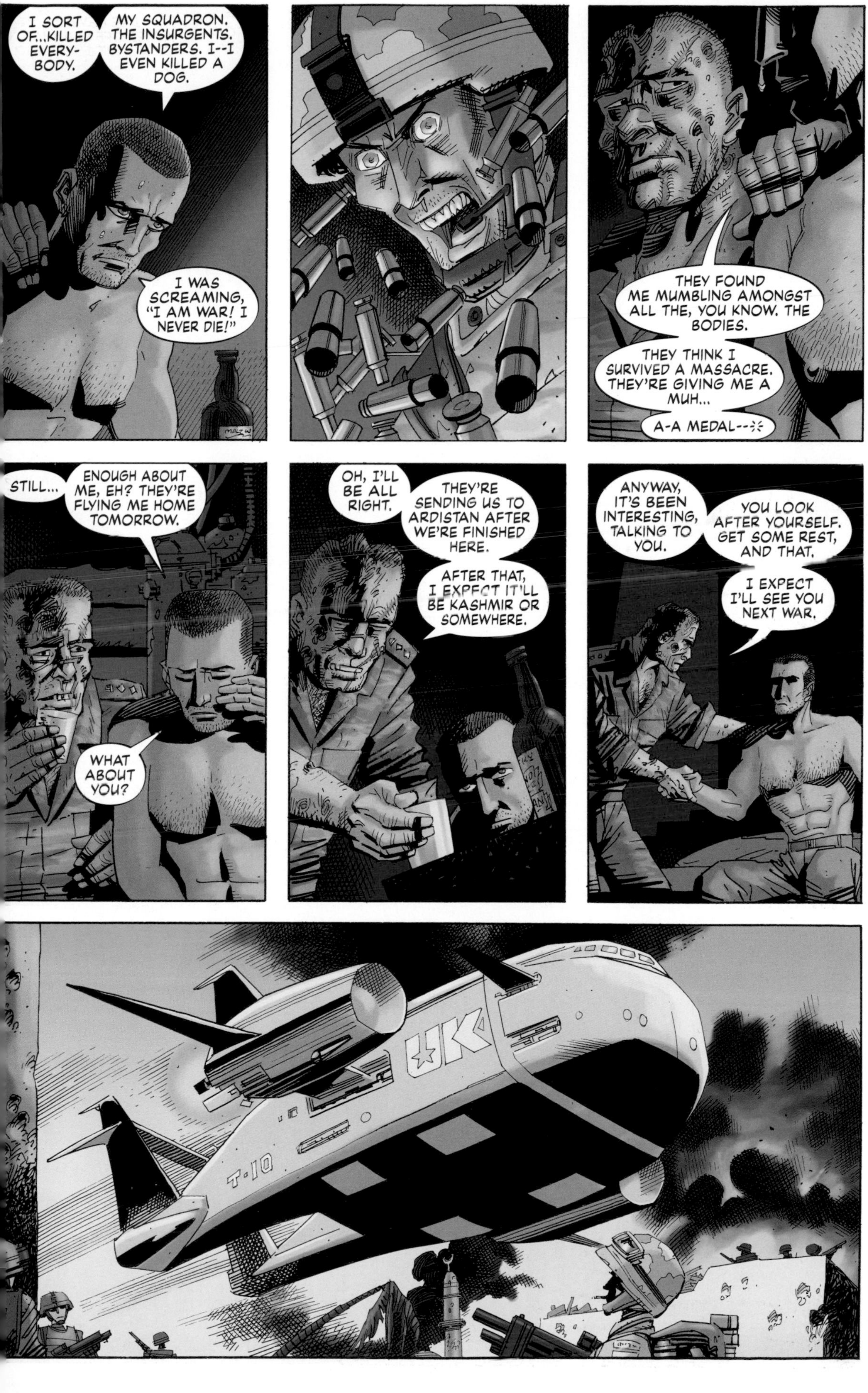

I SORT OF...KILLED EVERY-BODY.
MY SQUADRON. THE INSURGENTS. BYSTANDERS. I--I EVEN KILLED A DOG.
I WAS SCREAMING, "I AM WAR! I NEVER DIE!"
THEY FOUND ME MUMBLING AMONGST ALL THE, YOU KNOW. THE BODIES.
THEY THINK I SURVIVED A MASSACRE. THEY'RE GIVING ME A MUH...
A-A MEDAL--
STILL...
ENOUGH ABOUT ME, EH? THEY'RE FLYING ME HOME TOMORROW.
WHAT ABOUT YOU?
OH, I'LL BE ALL RIGHT.
THEY'RE SENDING US TO ARDISTAN AFTER WE'RE FINISHED HERE.
AFTER THAT, I EXPECT IT'LL BE KASHMIR OR SOMEWHERE.
ANYWAY, IT'S BEEN INTERESTING, TALKING TO YOU.
YOU LOOK AFTER YOURSELF. GET SOME REST, AND THAT.
I EXPECT I'LL SEE YOU NEXT WAR.
UK
T-10

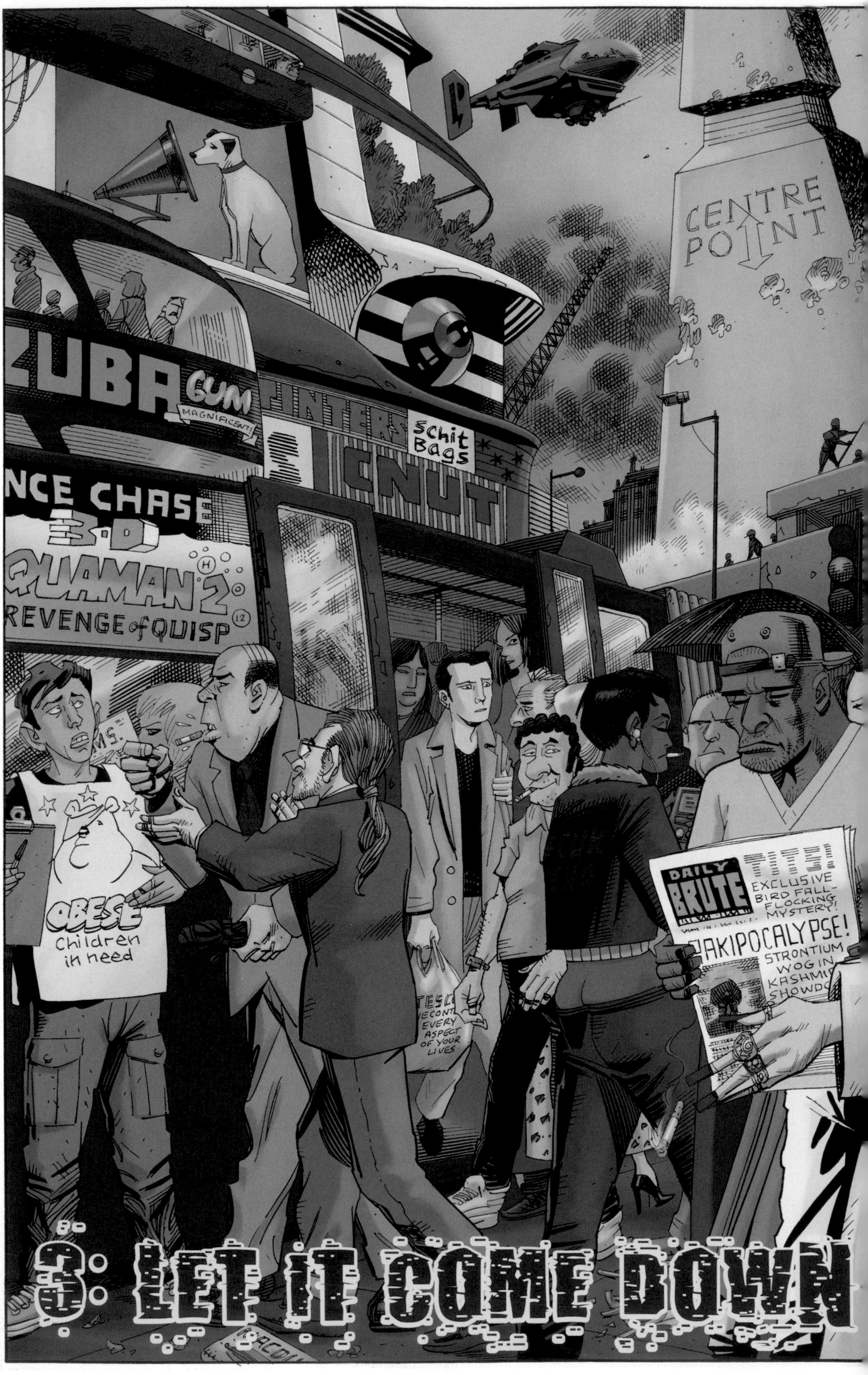
CENTRE POINT
GUM
MAGNIFICENT!
Schit Bags
CNUT
NCE CHASE
3-D
QUAMAN 2
REVENGE of QUISP
OBESE
Children in need
TESCO
WE CONTROL EVERY ASPECT OF YOUR LIVES
DAILY BRUTE
TITS!
EXCLUSIVE
BIRD FALL-FLOCKING MYSTERY!
PAKIPOCALYPSE!
STRONTIUM
WOG IN
KASHMIR
SHOWDO
3: LET IT COME DOWN

OH, WHO CARES?
The NEW album FROM DRIVESHAFT

The DRUM 'N' BASSMENT

ASS in ATTACK!!

FUR-Q IN THE HOUSE

N.W.H REUNION SCRATCH MY BITCH

CRIB

MASSIVE GENIUS

REST ROOMS

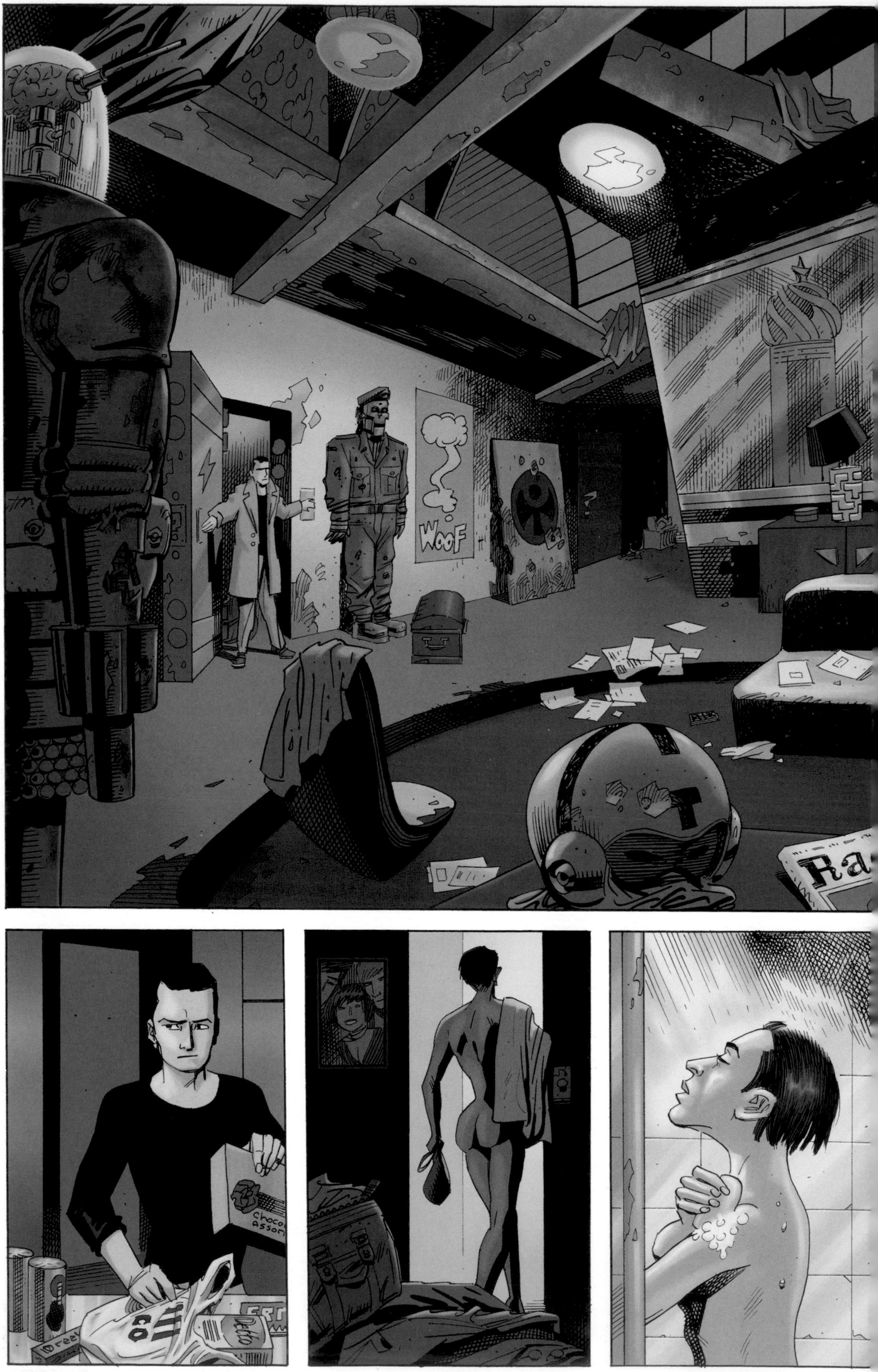
WOOF

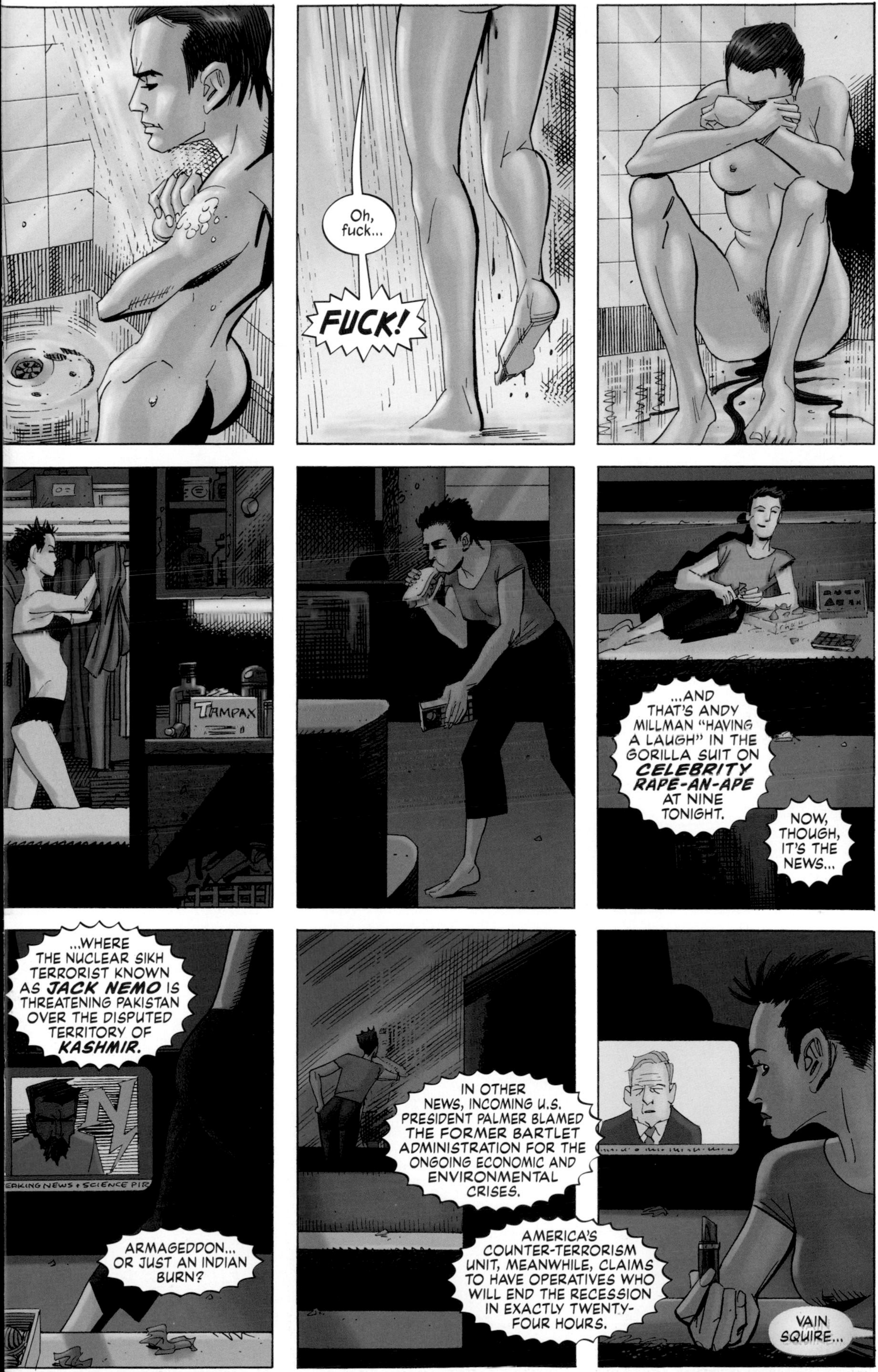

Oh, fuck...
FUCK!
TAMPAX
...AND THAT'S ANDY MILLMAN "HAVING A LAUGH" IN THE GORILLA SUIT ON CELEBRITY RAPE-AN-APE AT NINE TONIGHT.
NOW, THOUGH, IT'S THE NEWS...
...WHERE THE NUCLEAR SIKH TERRORIST KNOWN AS JACK NEMO IS THREATENING PAKISTAN OVER THE DISPUTED TERRITORY OF KASHMIR.
EAKING NEWS + SCIENCE PIR
ARMAGEDDON... OR JUST AN INDIAN BURN?
IN OTHER NEWS, INCOMING U.S. PRESIDENT PALMER BLAMED THE FORMER BARTLET ADMINISTRATION FOR THE ONGOING ECONOMIC AND ENVIRONMENTAL CRISES.
AMERICA'S COUNTER-TERRORISM UNIT, MEANWHILE, CLAIMS TO HAVE OPERATIVES WHO WILL END THE RECESSION IN EXACTLY TWENTY-FOUR HOURS.
VAIN SQUIRE...

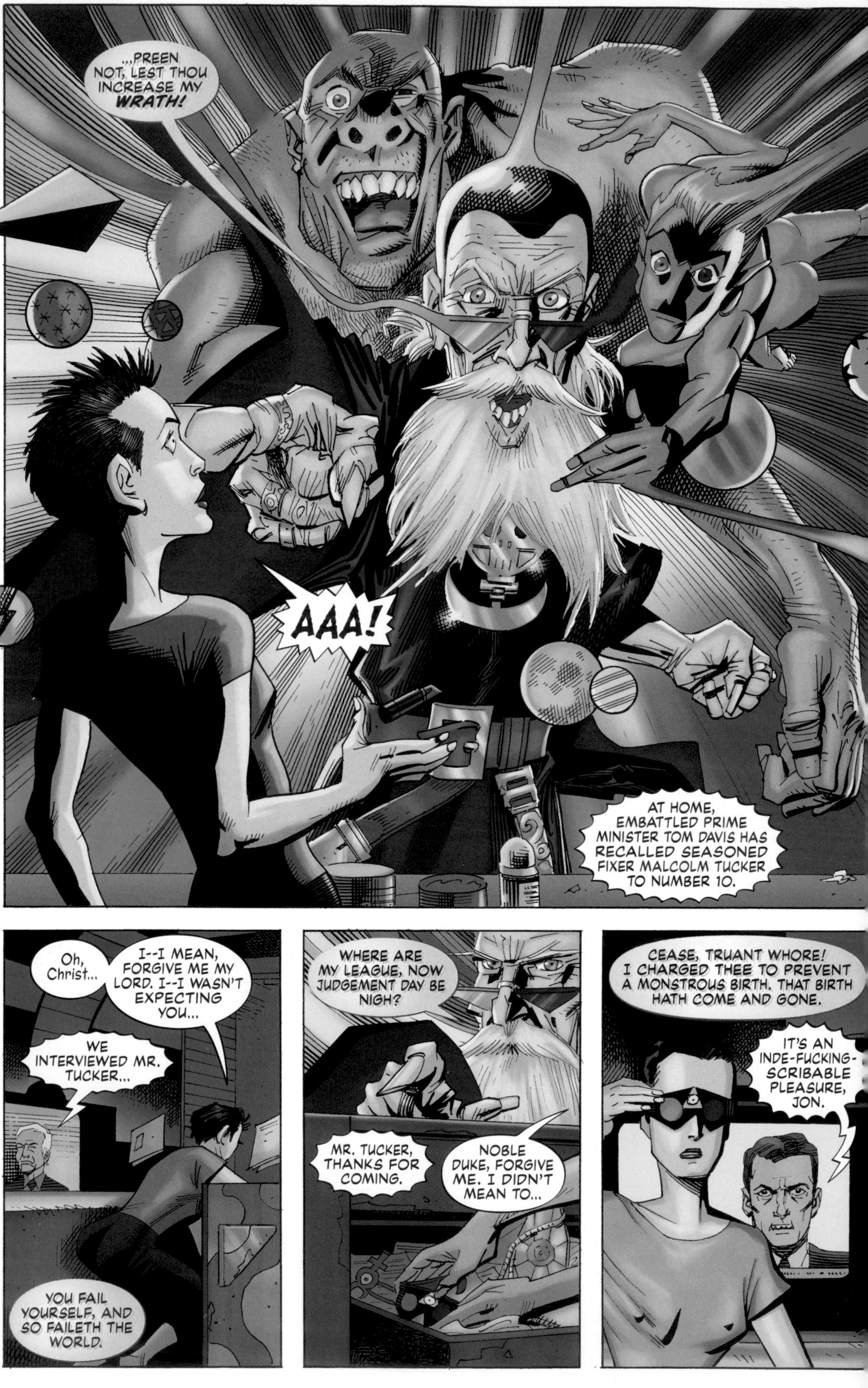
...PREEN NOT, LEST THOU INCREASE MY *WRATH!*
AAA!
AT HOME, EMBATTLED PRIME MINISTER TOM DAVIS HAS RECALLED SEASONED FIXER MALCOLM TUCKER TO NUMBER 10.
Oh, Christ...
I--I MEAN, FORGIVE ME MY LORD. I--I WASN'T EXPECTING YOU...
WE INTERVIEWED MR. TUCKER...
YOU FAIL YOURSELF, AND SO FAILETH THE WORLD.
WHERE ARE MY LEAGUE, NOW JUDGEMENT DAY BE NIGH?
MR. TUCKER, THANKS FOR COMING.
NOBLE DUKE, FORGIVE ME. I DIDN'T MEAN TO...
CEASE, TRUANT WHORE! I CHARGED THEE TO PREVENT A MONSTROUS BIRTH. THAT BIRTH HATH COME AND GONE.
IT'S AN INDE-FUCKING-SCRIBABLE PLEASURE, JON.

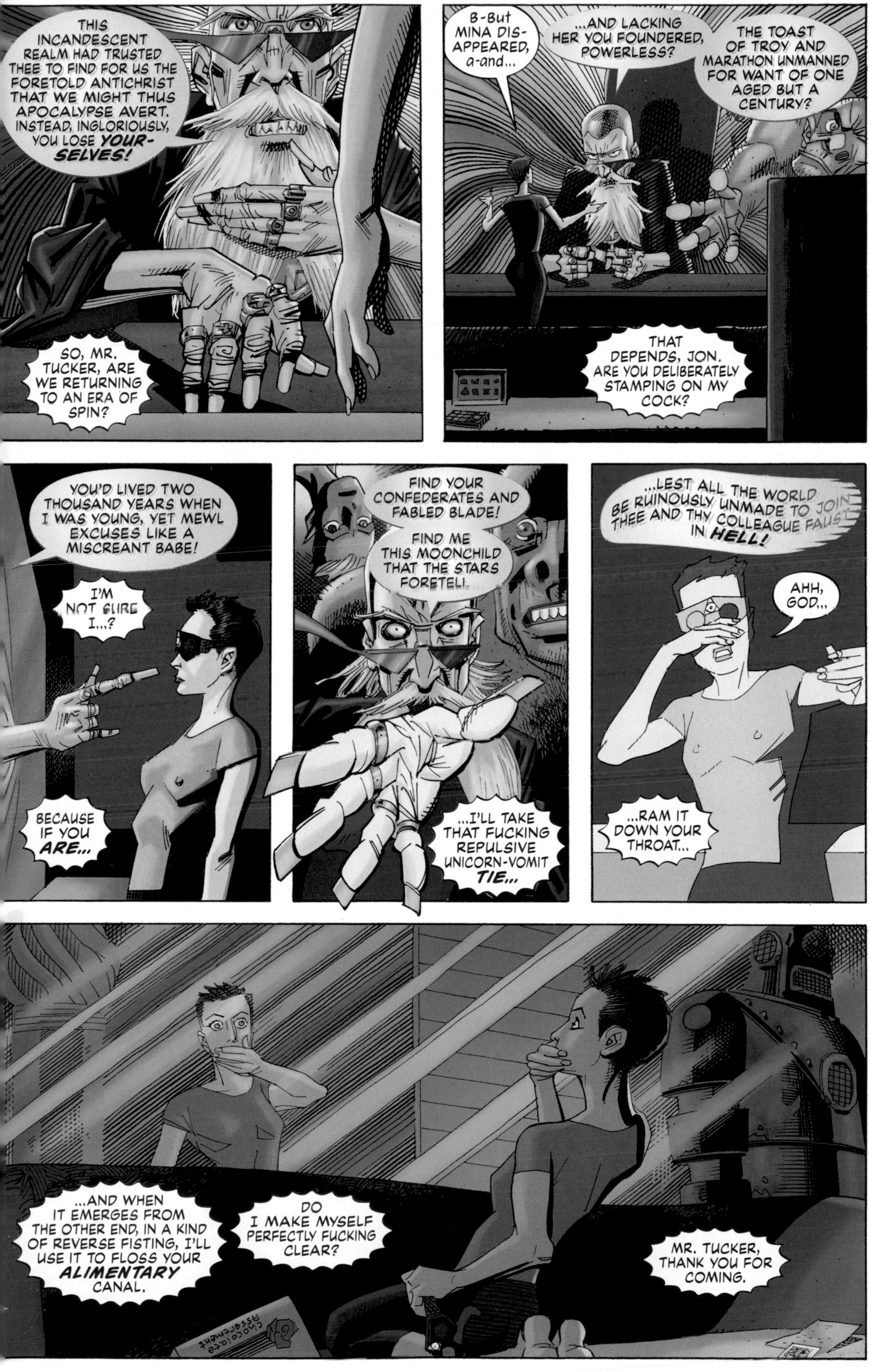
THIS INCANDESCENT REALM HAD TRUSTED THEE TO FIND FOR US THE FORETOLD ANTICHRIST THAT WE MIGHT THUS APOCALYPSE AVERT. INSTEAD, INGLORIOUSLY, YOU LOSE *YOURSELVES!*
SO, MR. TUCKER, ARE WE RETURNING TO AN ERA OF SPIN?
B-But MINA DISAPPEARED, a-and...
...AND LACKING HER YOU FOUNDERED, POWERLESS?
THE TOAST OF TROY AND MARATHON UNMANNED FOR WANT OF ONE AGED BUT A CENTURY?
THAT DEPENDS, JON. ARE YOU DELIBERATELY STAMPING ON MY COCK?
YOU'D LIVED TWO THOUSAND YEARS WHEN I WAS YOUNG, YET MEWL EXCUSES LIKE A MISCREANT BABE!
I'M NOT SURE I...?
BECAUSE IF YOU *ARE...*
FIND YOUR CONFEDERATES AND FABLED BLADE!
FIND ME THIS MOONCHILD THAT THE STARS FORETELL...
...I'LL TAKE THAT FUCKING REPULSIVE UNICORN-VOMIT *TIE...*
...LEST ALL THE WORLD BE RUINOUSLY UNMADE TO JOIN THEE AND THY COLLEAGUE FAUST IN *HELL!*
AHH, GOD...
...RAM IT DOWN YOUR THROAT...
...AND WHEN IT EMERGES FROM THE OTHER END, IN A KIND OF REVERSE FISTING, I'LL USE IT TO FLOSS YOUR *ALIMENTARY* CANAL.
DO I MAKE MYSELF PERFECTLY FUCKING CLEAR?
MR. TUCKER, THANK YOU FOR COMING.

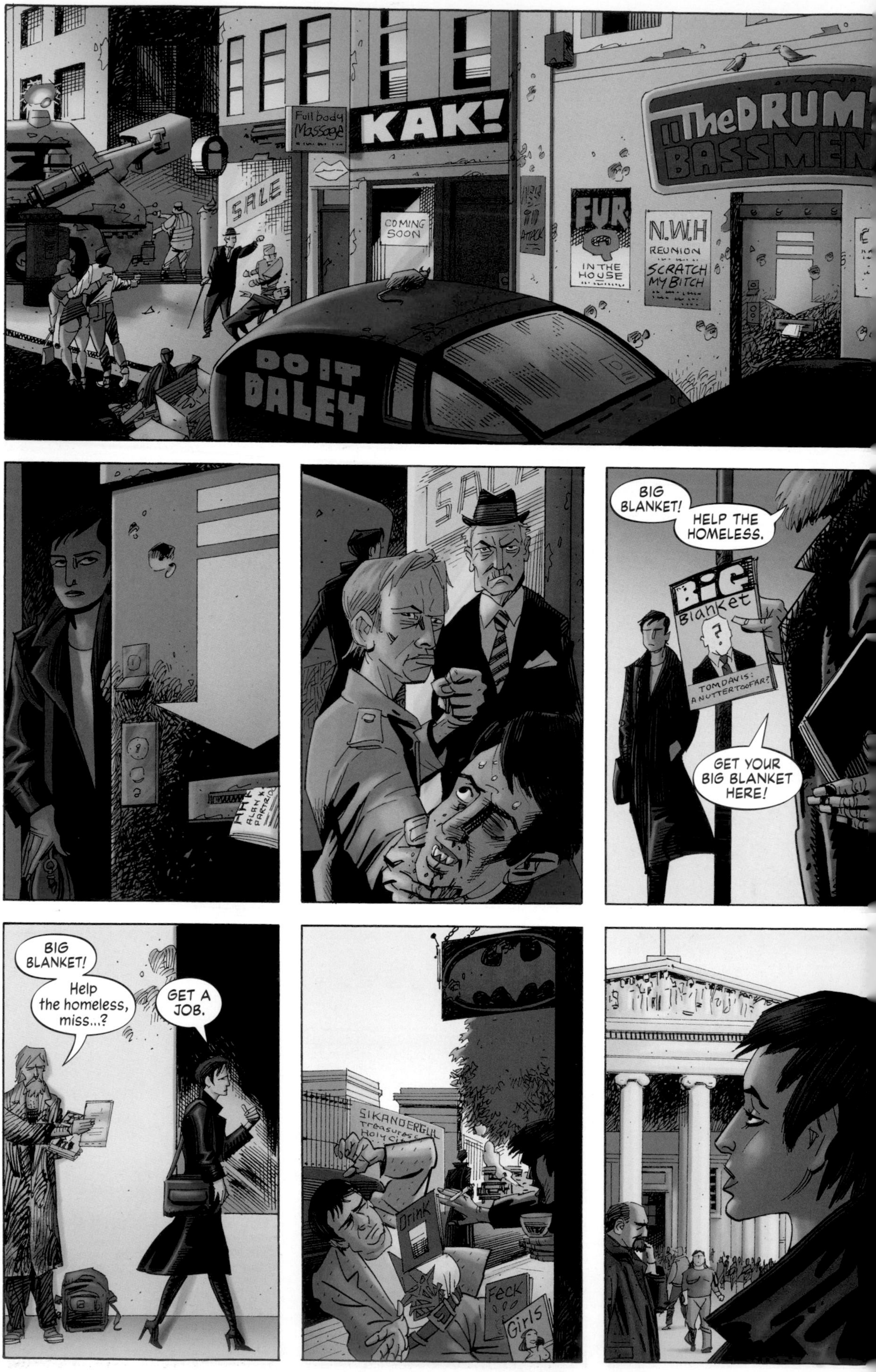
Full body Massage
KAK!
TheDRUM
BASSMEN
SALE
COMING SOON
FUR Q IN THE HOUSE
N.W.H REUNION
SCRATCH MY BITCH
DO IT DALEY
BIG BLANKET!
HELP THE HOMELESS.
Big Blanket
TOM DAVIS: A NUTTER TOO FAR?
GET YOUR BIG BLANKET HERE!
BIG BLANKET!
Help the homeless, miss...?
GET A JOB.
SIKANDERGUL
Drink
Feck
Girls

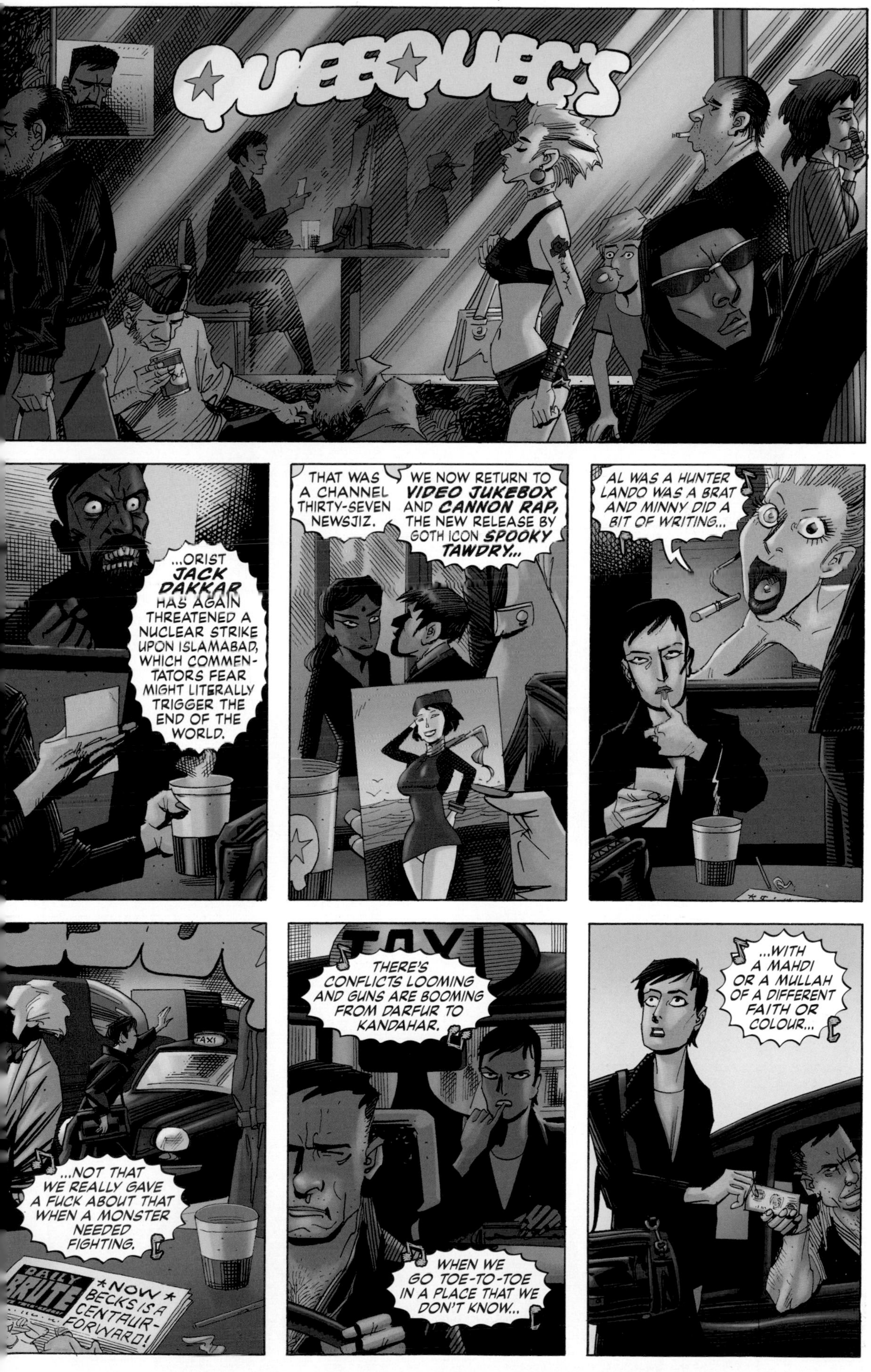
QUEEQUEG'S
...ORIST JACK DAKKAR HAS AGAIN THREATENED A NUCLEAR STRIKE UPON ISLAMABAD, WHICH COMMENTATORS FEAR MIGHT LITERALLY TRIGGER THE END OF THE WORLD.
THAT WAS A CHANNEL THIRTY-SEVEN NEWSJIZ.
WE NOW RETURN TO VIDEO JUKEBOX AND CANNON RAP, THE NEW RELEASE BY GOTH ICON SPOOKY TAWDRY...
AL WAS A HUNTER LANDO WAS A BRAT AND MINNY DID A BIT OF WRITING...
TAXI
...NOT THAT WE REALLY GAVE A FUCK ABOUT THAT WHEN A MONSTER NEEDED FIGHTING.
DAILY BRUTE
NOW BECKS IS A CENTAUR-FORWARD!
TAXI
THERE'S CONFLICTS LOOMING AND GUNS ARE BOOMING FROM DARFUR TO KANDAHAR.
WHEN WE GO TOE-TO-TOE IN A PLACE THAT WE DON'T KNOW...
...WITH A MAHDI OR A MULLAH OF A DIFFERENT FAITH OR COLOUR...

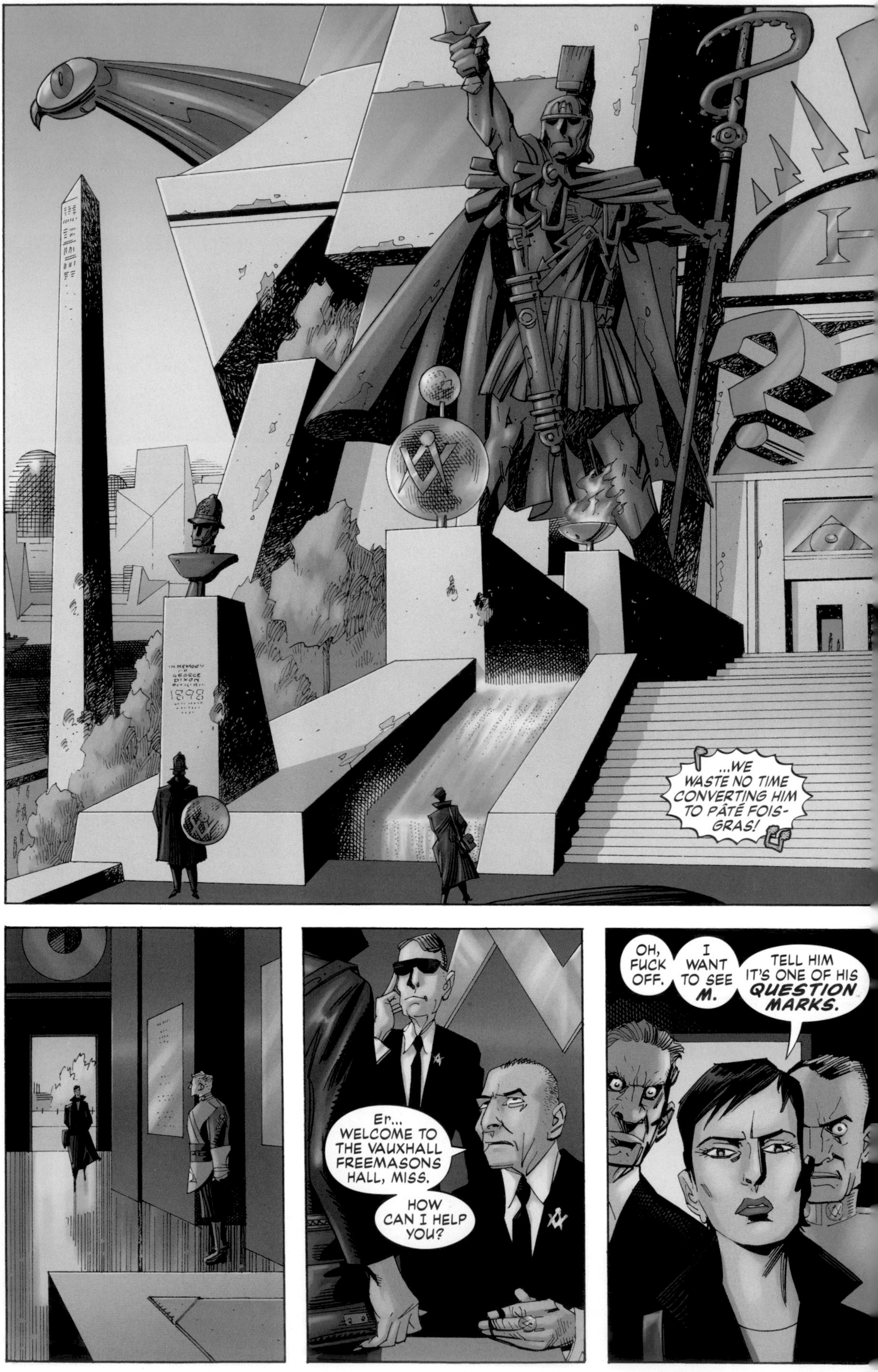
IN MEMORY OF GEORGE DIXON
1898
...WE WASTE NO TIME CONVERTING HIM TO PÂTÉ FOIS-GRAS!
Er... WELCOME TO THE VAUXHALL FREEMASONS HALL, MISS.
HOW CAN I HELP YOU?
OH, FUCK OFF.
I WANT TO SEE M.
TELL HIM IT'S ONE OF HIS QUESTION MARKS.

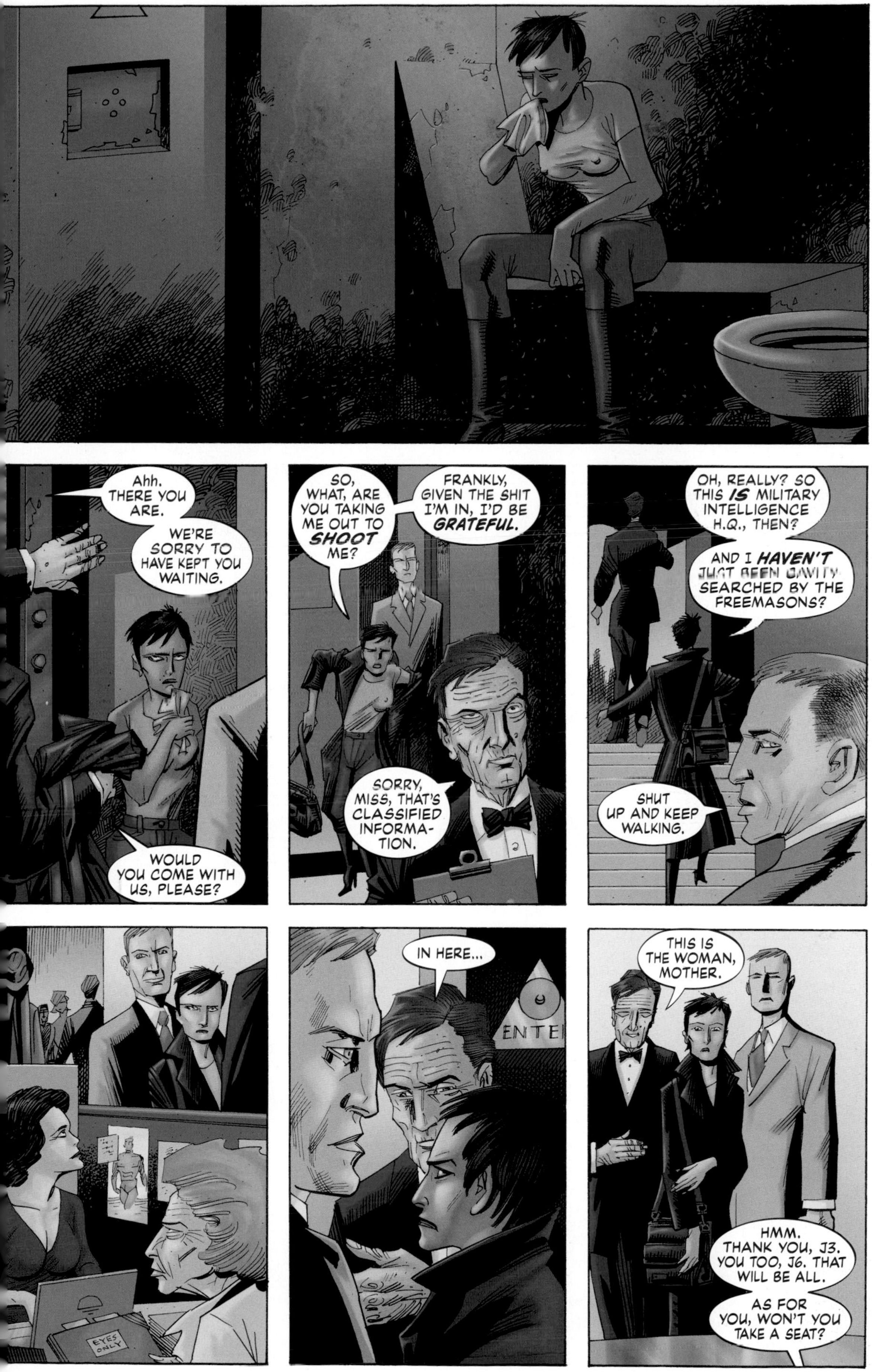
Ahh. THERE YOU ARE.
WE'RE SORRY TO HAVE KEPT YOU WAITING.
WOULD YOU COME WITH US, PLEASE?
SO, WHAT, ARE YOU TAKING ME OUT TO SHOOT ME?
FRANKLY, GIVEN THE SHIT I'M IN, I'D BE GRATEFUL.
SORRY, MISS, THAT'S CLASSIFIED INFORMA-TION.
OH, REALLY? SO THIS IS MILITARY INTELLIGENCE H.Q., THEN?
AND I HAVEN'T JUST BEEN CAVITY SEARCHED BY THE FREEMASONS?
SHUT UP AND KEEP WALKING.
EYES ONLY
IN HERE...
ENTE
THIS IS THE WOMAN, MOTHER.
HMM. THANK YOU, J3. YOU TOO, J6. THAT WILL BE ALL.
AS FOR YOU, WON'T YOU TAKE A SEAT?

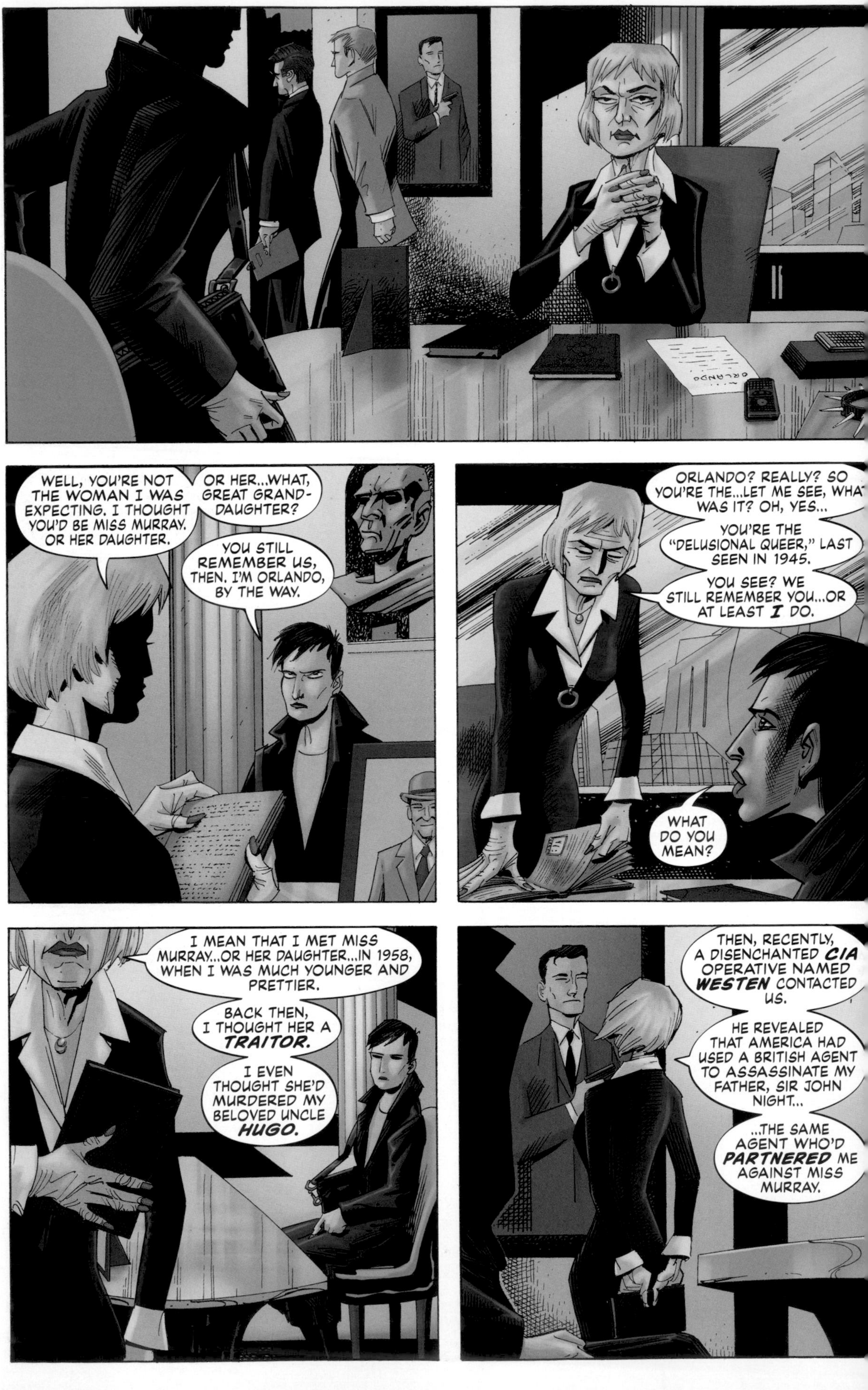
ORLANDO
WELL, YOU'RE NOT THE WOMAN I WAS EXPECTING. I THOUGHT YOU'D BE MISS MURRAY. OR HER DAUGHTER.
OR HER...WHAT, GREAT GRAND-DAUGHTER?
YOU STILL REMEMBER US, THEN. I'M ORLANDO, BY THE WAY.
ORLANDO? REALLY? SO YOU'RE THE...LET ME SEE, WHAT WAS IT? OH, YES...
YOU'RE THE "DELUSIONAL QUEER," LAST SEEN IN 1945.
YOU SEE? WE STILL REMEMBER YOU...OR AT LEAST *I* DO.
WHAT DO YOU MEAN?
I MEAN THAT I MET MISS MURRAY...OR HER DAUGHTER...IN 1958, WHEN I WAS MUCH YOUNGER AND PRETTIER.
BACK THEN, I THOUGHT HER A ***TRAITOR.***
I EVEN THOUGHT SHE'D MURDERED MY BELOVED UNCLE ***HUGO.***
THEN, RECENTLY, A DISENCHANTED ***CIA*** OPERATIVE NAMED ***WESTEN*** CONTACTED US.
HE REVEALED THAT AMERICA HAD USED A BRITISH AGENT TO ASSASSINATE MY FATHER, SIR JOHN NIGHT...
...THE SAME AGENT WHO'D ***PARTNERED*** ME AGAINST MISS MURRAY.

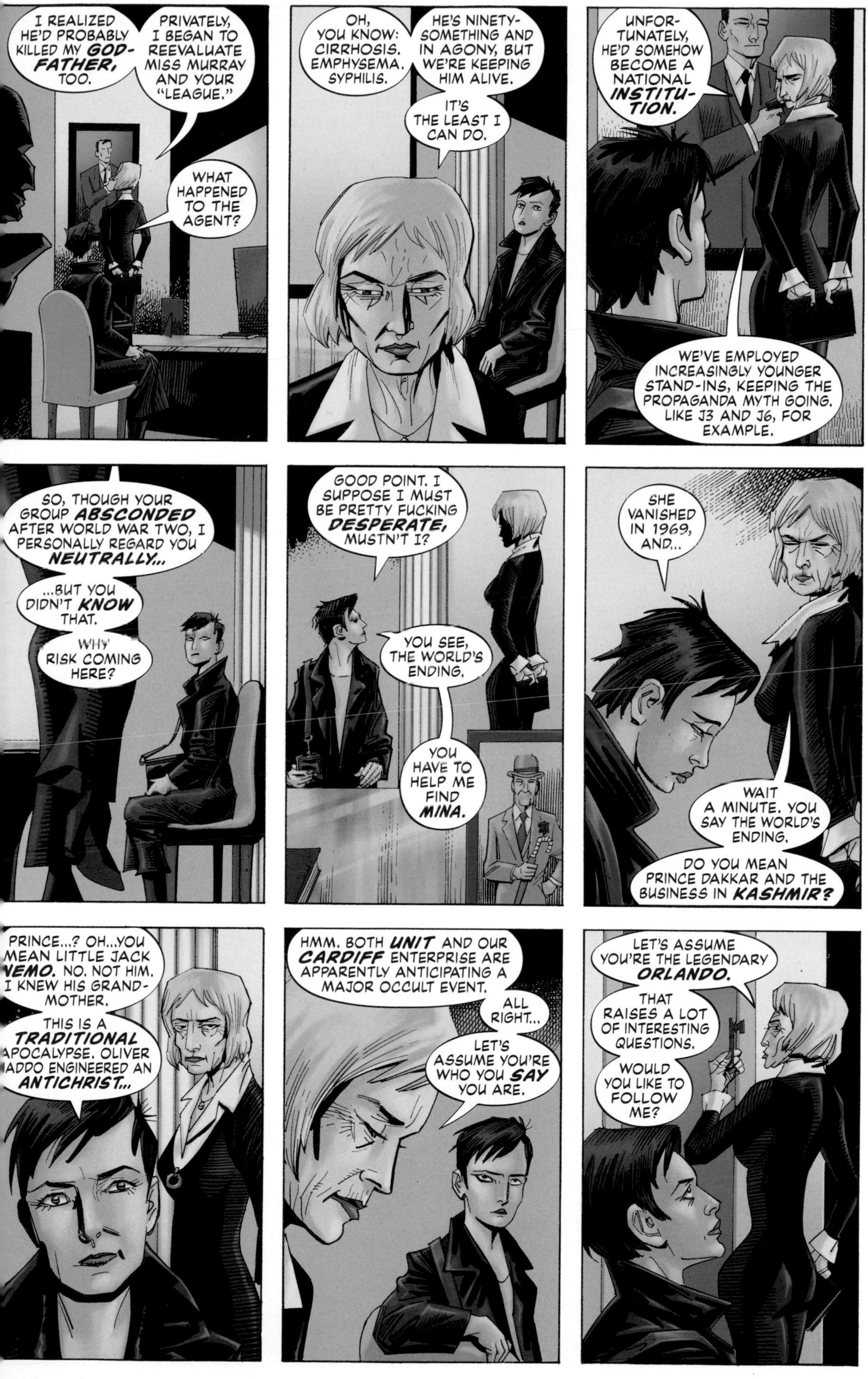
I REALIZED HE'D PROBABLY KILLED MY GODFATHER, TOO.
PRIVATELY, I BEGAN TO REEVALUATE MISS MURRAY AND YOUR "LEAGUE."
WHAT HAPPENED TO THE AGENT?
OH, YOU KNOW: CIRRHOSIS. EMPHYSEMA. SYPHILIS.
HE'S NINETY-SOMETHING AND IN AGONY, BUT WE'RE KEEPING HIM ALIVE.
IT'S THE LEAST I CAN DO.
UNFORTUNATELY, HE'D SOMEHOW BECOME A NATIONAL INSTITUTION.
WE'VE EMPLOYED INCREASINGLY YOUNGER STAND-INS, KEEPING THE PROPAGANDA MYTH GOING. LIKE J3 AND J6, FOR EXAMPLE.
SO, THOUGH YOUR GROUP ABSCONDED AFTER WORLD WAR TWO, I PERSONALLY REGARD YOU NEUTRALLY...
...BUT YOU DIDN'T KNOW THAT.
WHY RISK COMING HERE?
GOOD POINT. I SUPPOSE I MUST BE PRETTY FUCKING DESPERATE, MUSTN'T I?
YOU SEE, THE WORLD'S ENDING.
YOU HAVE TO HELP ME FIND MINA.
SHE VANISHED IN 1969, AND...
WAIT A MINUTE. YOU SAY THE WORLD'S ENDING.
DO YOU MEAN PRINCE DAKKAR AND THE BUSINESS IN KASHMIR?
PRINCE...? OH...YOU MEAN LITTLE JACK NEMO. NO. NOT HIM. I KNEW HIS GRANDMOTHER.
THIS IS A TRADITIONAL APOCALYPSE. OLIVER HADDO ENGINEERED AN ANTICHRIST...
HMM. BOTH UNIT AND OUR CARDIFF ENTERPRISE ARE APPARENTLY ANTICIPATING A MAJOR OCCULT EVENT.
ALL RIGHT...
LET'S ASSUME YOU'RE WHO YOU SAY YOU ARE.
LET'S ASSUME YOU'RE THE LEGENDARY ORLANDO.
THAT RAISES A LOT OF INTERESTING QUESTIONS.
WOULD YOU LIKE TO FOLLOW ME?

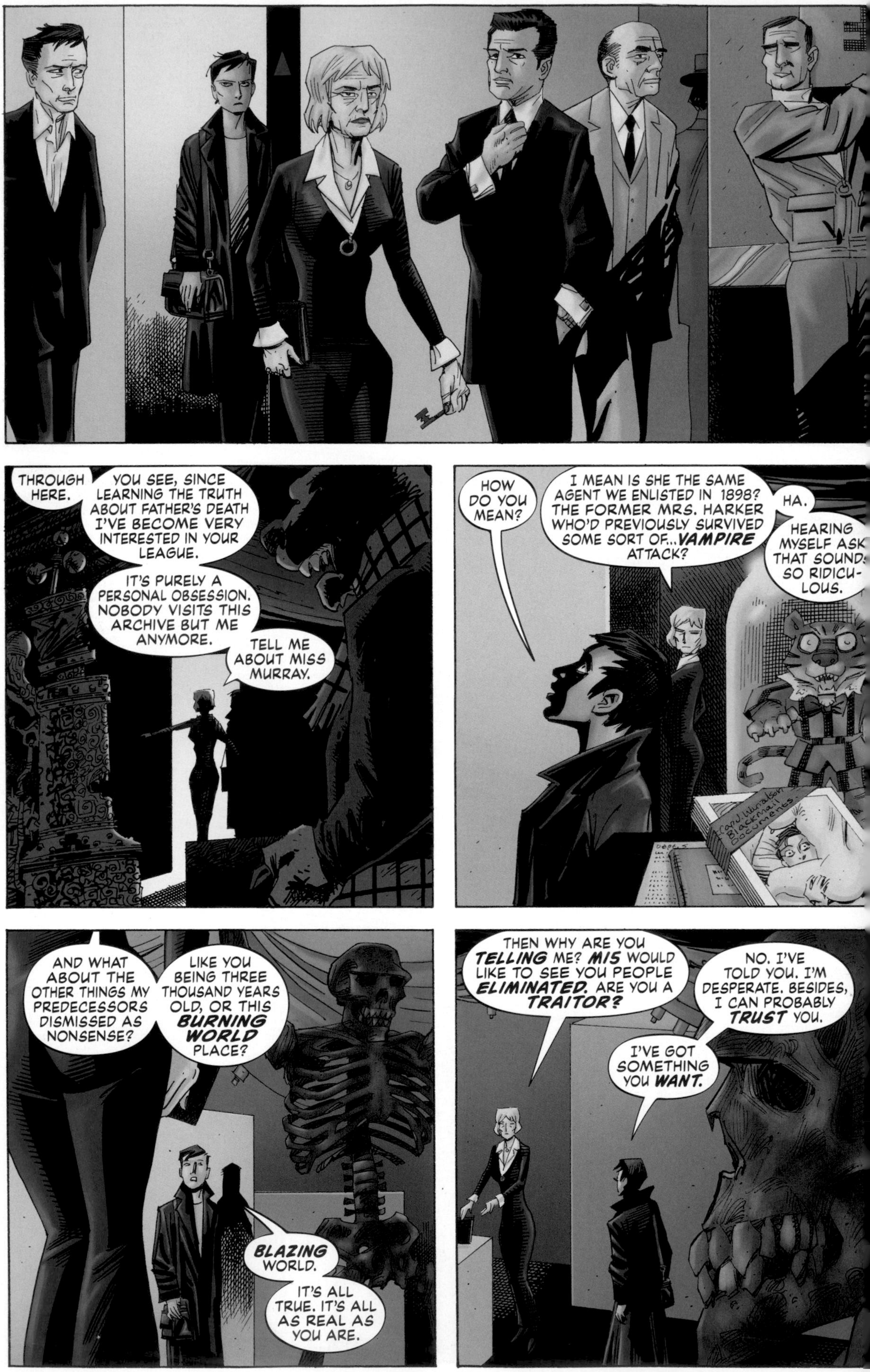
THROUGH HERE.
YOU SEE, SINCE LEARNING THE TRUTH ABOUT FATHER'S DEATH I'VE BECOME VERY INTERESTED IN YOUR LEAGUE.
IT'S PURELY A PERSONAL OBSESSION. NOBODY VISITS THIS ARCHIVE BUT ME ANYMORE.
TELL ME ABOUT MISS MURRAY.
HOW DO YOU MEAN?
I MEAN IS SHE THE SAME AGENT WE ENLISTED IN 1898? THE FORMER MRS. HARKER WHO'D PREVIOUSLY SURVIVED SOME SORT OF...VAMPIRE ATTACK?
HA.
HEARING MYSELF ASK THAT SOUND SO RIDICU-LOUS.
AND WHAT ABOUT THE OTHER THINGS MY PREDECESSORS DISMISSED AS NONSENSE?
LIKE YOU BEING THREE THOUSAND YEARS OLD, OR THIS BURNING WORLD PLACE?
BLAZING WORLD.
IT'S ALL TRUE. IT'S ALL AS REAL AS YOU ARE.
THEN WHY ARE YOU TELLING ME? MI5 WOULD LIKE TO SEE YOU PEOPLE ELIMINATED. ARE YOU A TRAITOR?
NO. I'VE TOLD YOU. I'M DESPERATE. BESIDES, I CAN PROBABLY TRUST YOU.
I'VE GOT SOMETHING YOU WANT.

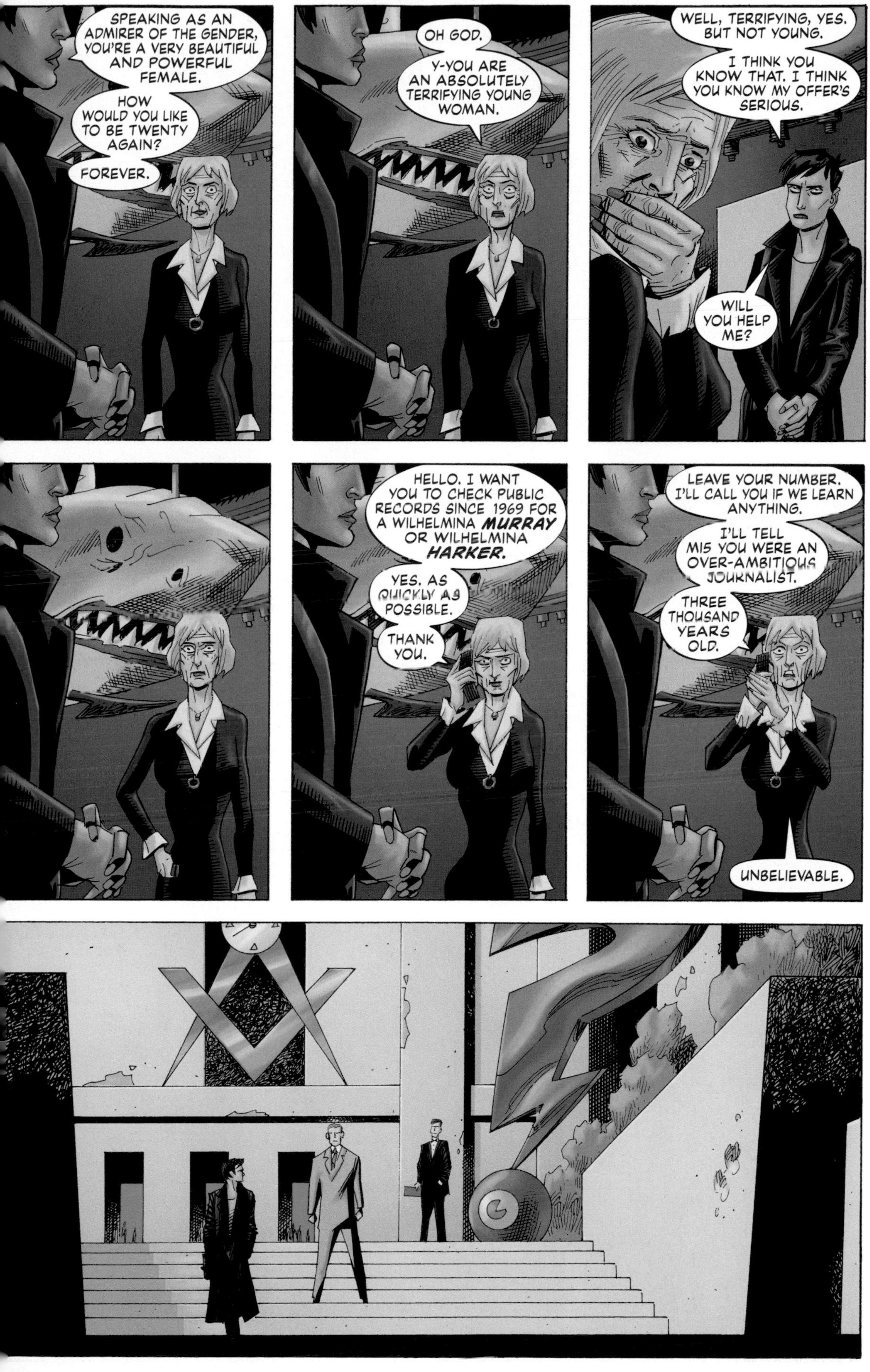
SPEAKING AS AN ADMIRER OF THE GENDER, YOU'RE A VERY BEAUTIFUL AND POWERFUL FEMALE.
HOW WOULD YOU LIKE TO BE TWENTY AGAIN?
FOREVER.
OH GOD.
Y-YOU ARE AN ABSOLUTELY TERRIFYING YOUNG WOMAN.
WELL, TERRIFYING, YES. BUT NOT YOUNG.
I THINK YOU KNOW THAT. I THINK YOU KNOW MY OFFER'S SERIOUS.
WILL YOU HELP ME?
HELLO. I WANT YOU TO CHECK PUBLIC RECORDS SINCE 1969 FOR A WILHELMINA **MURRAY** OR WILHELMINA **HARKER.**
YES. AS QUICKLY AS POSSIBLE.
THANK YOU.
LEAVE YOUR NUMBER. I'LL CALL YOU IF WE LEARN ANYTHING.
I'LL TELL MI5 YOU WERE AN OVER-AMBITIOUS JOURNALIST.
THREE THOUSAND YEARS OLD.
UNBELIEVABLE.

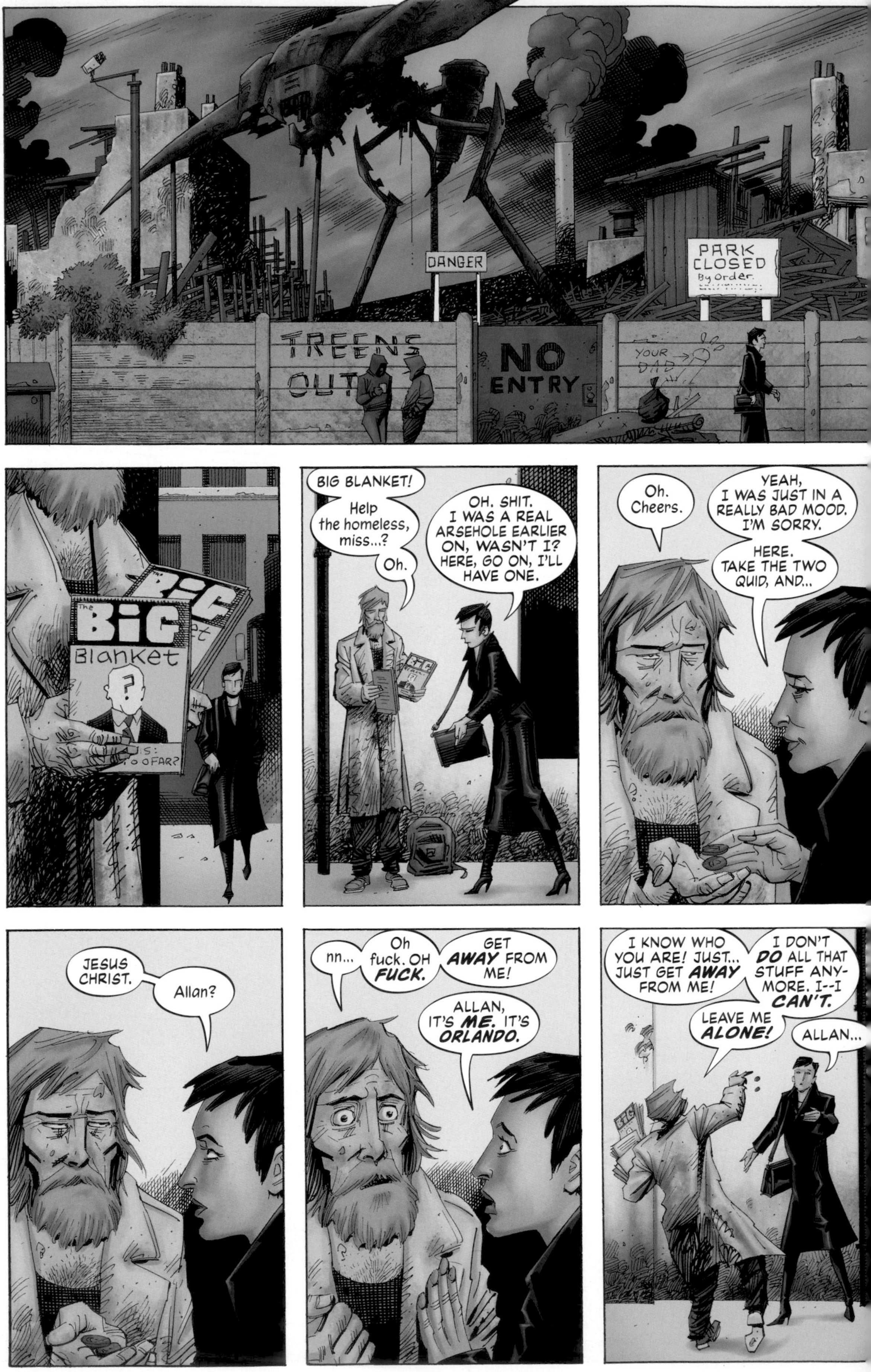
DANGER
PARK CLOSED By Order.
TREENS OUT
NO ENTRY
YOUR DAD
The BIG Blanket
BIG BLANKET!
Help the homeless, miss...?
Oh.
OH. SHIT. I WAS A REAL ARSEHOLE EARLIER ON, WASN'T I? HERE, GO ON, I'LL HAVE ONE.
Oh. Cheers.
YEAH, I WAS JUST IN A REALLY BAD MOOD. I'M SORRY.
HERE. TAKE THE TWO QUID, AND...
JESUS CHRIST.
Allan?
nn...
Oh fuck. OH FUCK.
GET AWAY FROM ME!
ALLAN, IT'S ME. IT'S ORLANDO.
I KNOW WHO YOU ARE! JUST... JUST GET AWAY FROM ME!
I DON'T DO ALL THAT STUFF ANY-MORE. I--I CAN'T.
LEAVE ME ALONE!
ALLAN...

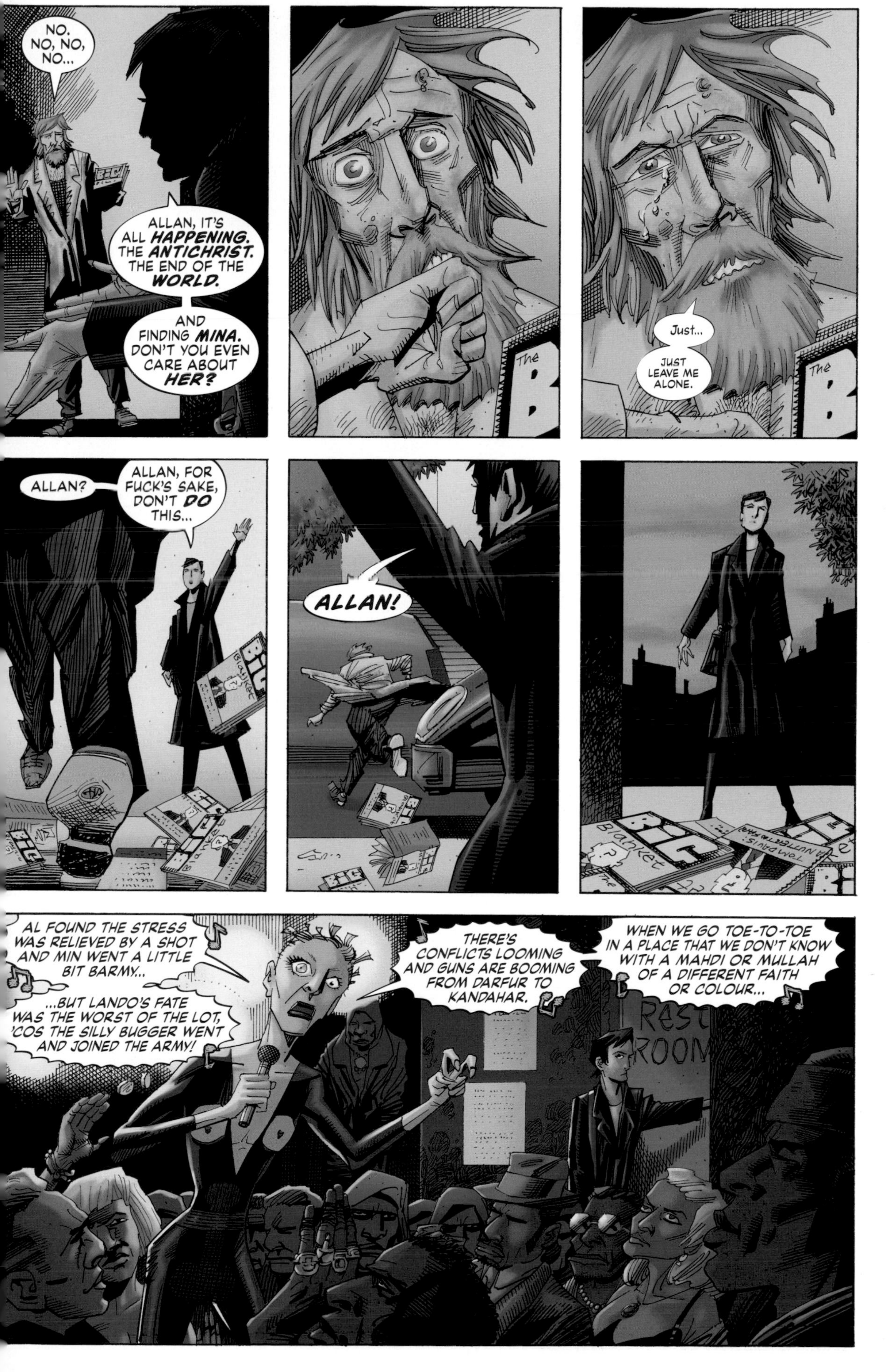

NO. NO, NO, NO...
ALLAN, IT'S ALL HAPPENING. THE ANTICHRIST. THE END OF THE WORLD.
AND FINDING MINA. DON'T YOU EVEN CARE ABOUT HER?
Just...
JUST LEAVE ME ALONE.
ALLAN?
ALLAN, FOR FUCK'S SAKE, DON'T DO THIS...
ALLAN!
AL FOUND THE STRESS WAS RELIEVED BY A SHOT AND MIN WENT A LITTLE BIT BARMY...
...BUT LANDO'S FATE WAS THE WORST OF THE LOT, 'COS THE SILLY BUGGER WENT AND JOINED THE ARMY!
THERE'S CONFLICTS LOOMING AND GUNS ARE BOOMING FROM DARFUR TO KANDAHAR.
WHEN WE GO TOE-TO-TOE IN A PLACE THAT WE DON'T KNOW WITH A MAHDI OR MULLAH OF A DIFFERENT FAITH OR COLOUR...
Rest ROOM

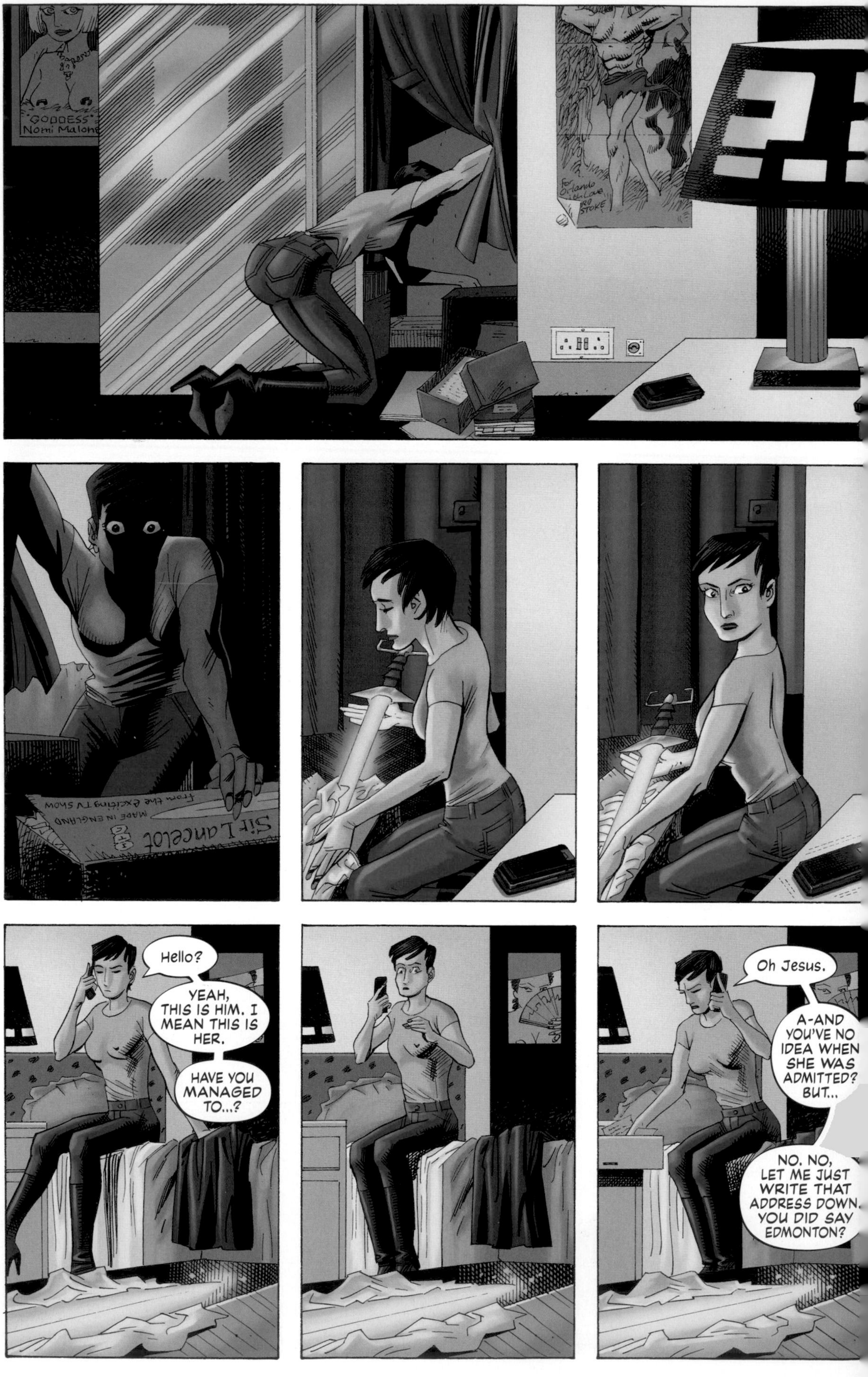

"GODDESS"
Nomi Malone
Sir Lancelot
MADE IN ENGLAND
from the exciting TV SHOW
Hello?
YEAH, THIS IS HIM. I MEAN THIS IS HER.
HAVE YOU MANAGED TO...?
Oh Jesus.
A-AND YOU'VE NO IDEA WHEN SHE WAS ADMITTED? BUT...
NO. NO, LET ME JUST WRITE THAT ADDRESS DOWN. YOU DID SAY EDMONTON?

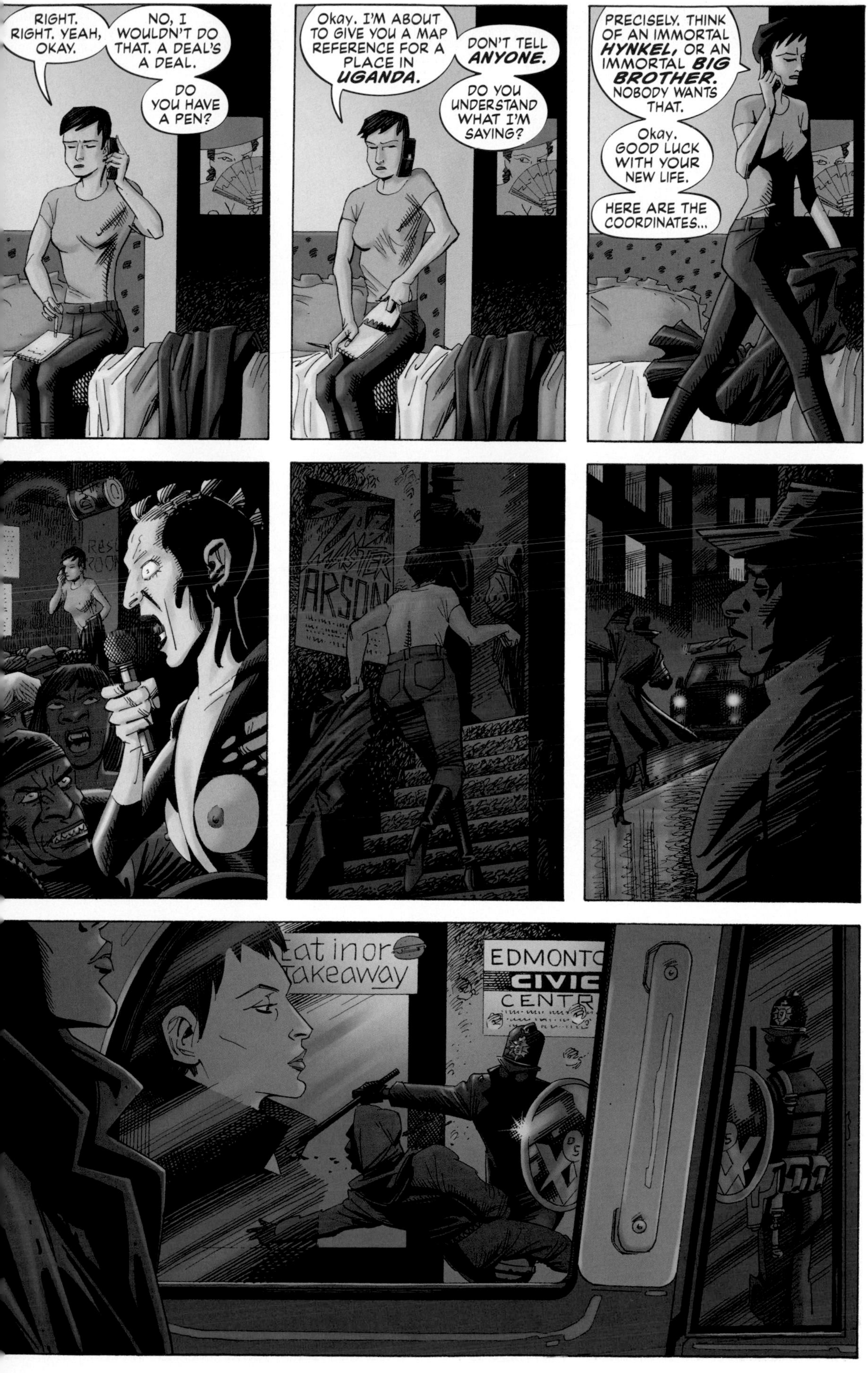

RIGHT. RIGHT. YEAH, OKAY.
NO, I WOULDN'T DO THAT. A DEAL'S A DEAL.
DO YOU HAVE A PEN?
Okay. I'M ABOUT TO GIVE YOU A MAP REFERENCE FOR A PLACE IN UGANDA.
DON'T TELL ANYONE.
DO YOU UNDERSTAND WHAT I'M SAYING?
PRECISELY. THINK OF AN IMMORTAL HYNKEL, OR AN IMMORTAL BIG BROTHER. NOBODY WANTS THAT.
Okay. GOOD LUCK WITH YOUR NEW LIFE.
HERE ARE THE COORDINATES...
ARSON
Eat in or Takeaway
EDMONTO
CIVIC
CENTR

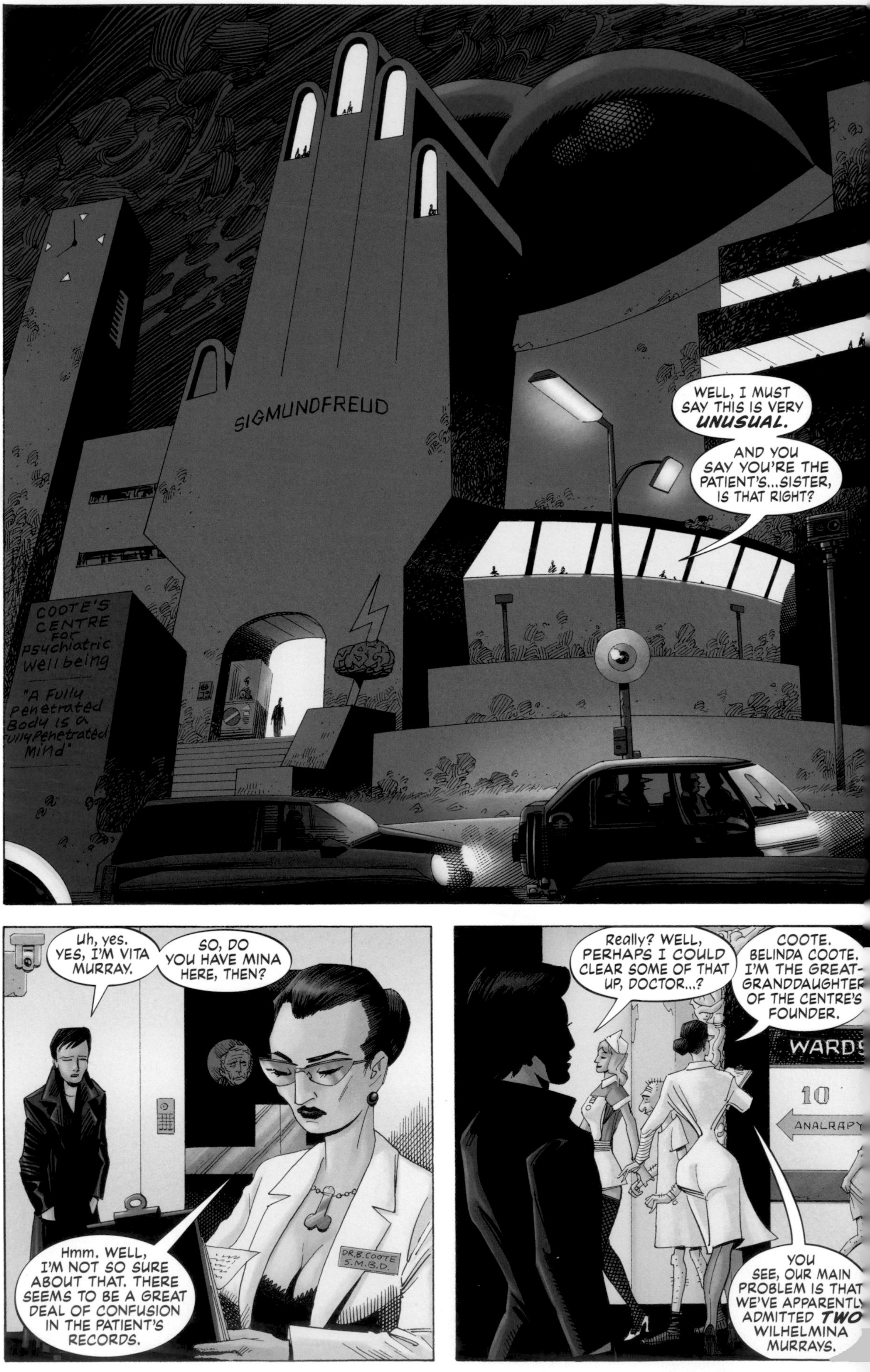
SIGMUNDFREUD
COOTE'S CENTRE for Psychiatric Well being
"A Fully Penetrated Body is a Fully Penetrated Mind"
WELL, I MUST SAY THIS IS VERY ***UNUSUAL.***
AND YOU SAY YOU'RE THE PATIENT'S...SISTER, IS THAT RIGHT?
Uh, yes. YES, I'M VITA MURRAY.
SO, DO YOU HAVE MINA HERE, THEN?
DR.B.COOTE S.M.B.D.
Hmm. WELL, I'M NOT SO SURE ABOUT THAT. THERE SEEMS TO BE A GREAT DEAL OF CONFUSION IN THE PATIENT'S RECORDS.
Really? WELL, PERHAPS I COULD CLEAR SOME OF THAT UP, DOCTOR...?
COOTE. BELINDA COOTE. I'M THE GREAT-GRANDDAUGHTER OF THE CENTRE'S FOUNDER.
WARDS
10
ANALRAPY
YOU SEE, OUR MAIN PROBLEM IS THAT WE'VE APPARENTLY ADMITTED ***TWO*** WILHELMINA MURRAYS.

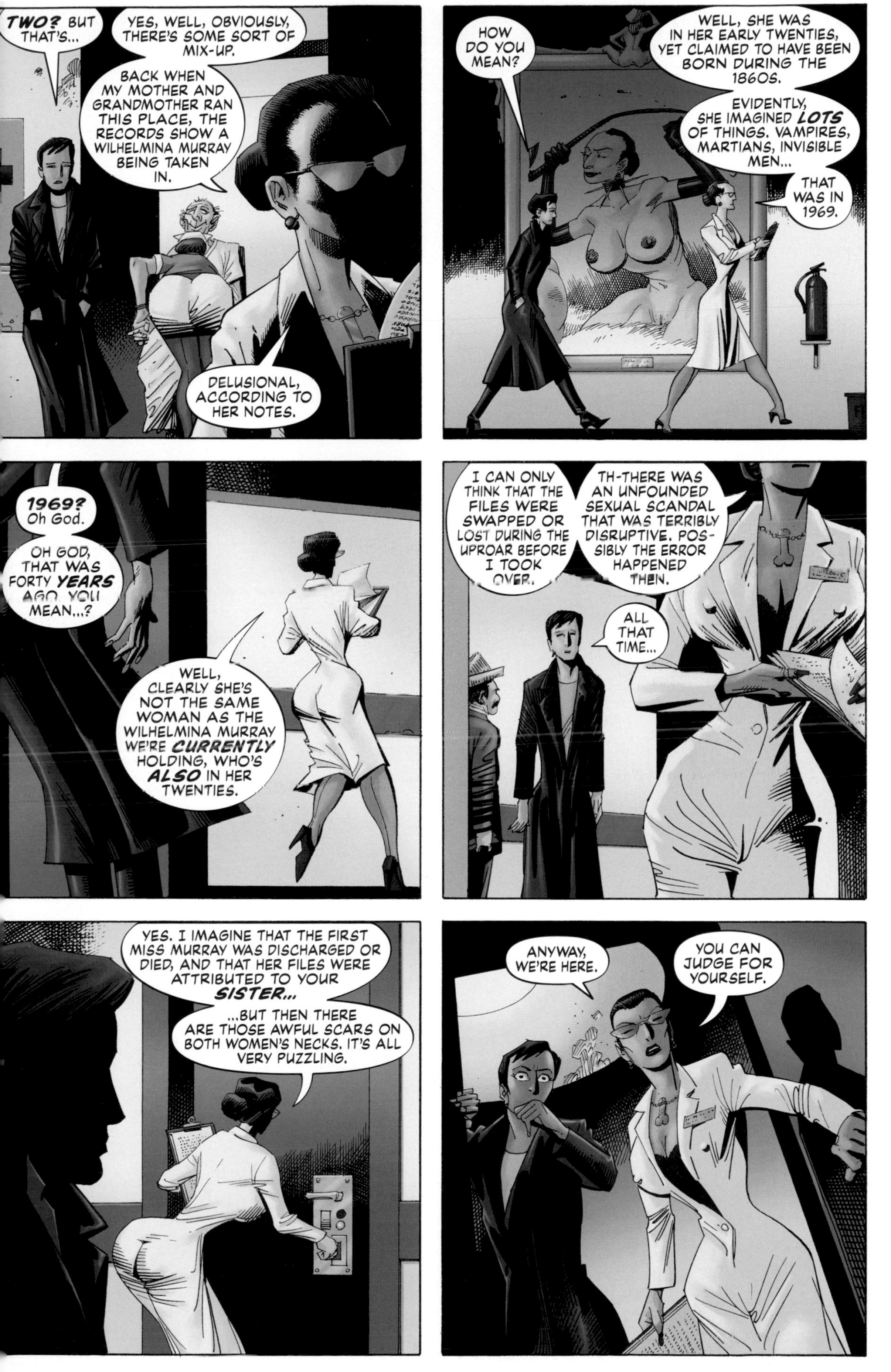
TWO? BUT THAT'S...
YES, WELL, OBVIOUSLY, THERE'S SOME SORT OF MIX-UP.
BACK WHEN MY MOTHER AND GRANDMOTHER RAN THIS PLACE, THE RECORDS SHOW A WILHELMINA MURRAY BEING TAKEN IN.
DELUSIONAL, ACCORDING TO HER NOTES.
HOW DO YOU MEAN?
WELL, SHE WAS IN HER EARLY TWENTIES, YET CLAIMED TO HAVE BEEN BORN DURING THE 1860S.
EVIDENTLY, SHE IMAGINED LOTS OF THINGS. VAMPIRES, MARTIANS, INVISIBLE MEN...
THAT WAS IN 1969.
1969? Oh God.
OH GOD, THAT WAS FORTY YEARS AGO. YOU MEAN...?
WELL, CLEARLY SHE'S NOT THE SAME WOMAN AS THE WILHELMINA MURRAY WE'RE CURRENTLY HOLDING, WHO'S ALSO IN HER TWENTIES.
I CAN ONLY THINK THAT THE FILES WERE SWAPPED OR LOST DURING THE UPROAR BEFORE I TOOK OVER.
TH-THERE WAS AN UNFOUNDED SEXUAL SCANDAL THAT WAS TERRIBLY DISRUPTIVE. POSSIBLY THE ERROR HAPPENED THEN.
ALL THAT TIME...
YES. I IMAGINE THAT THE FIRST MISS MURRAY WAS DISCHARGED OR DIED, AND THAT HER FILES WERE ATTRIBUTED TO YOUR SISTER...
...BUT THEN THERE ARE THOSE AWFUL SCARS ON BOTH WOMEN'S NECKS. IT'S ALL VERY PUZZLING.
ANYWAY, WE'RE HERE.
YOU CAN JUDGE FOR YOURSELF.

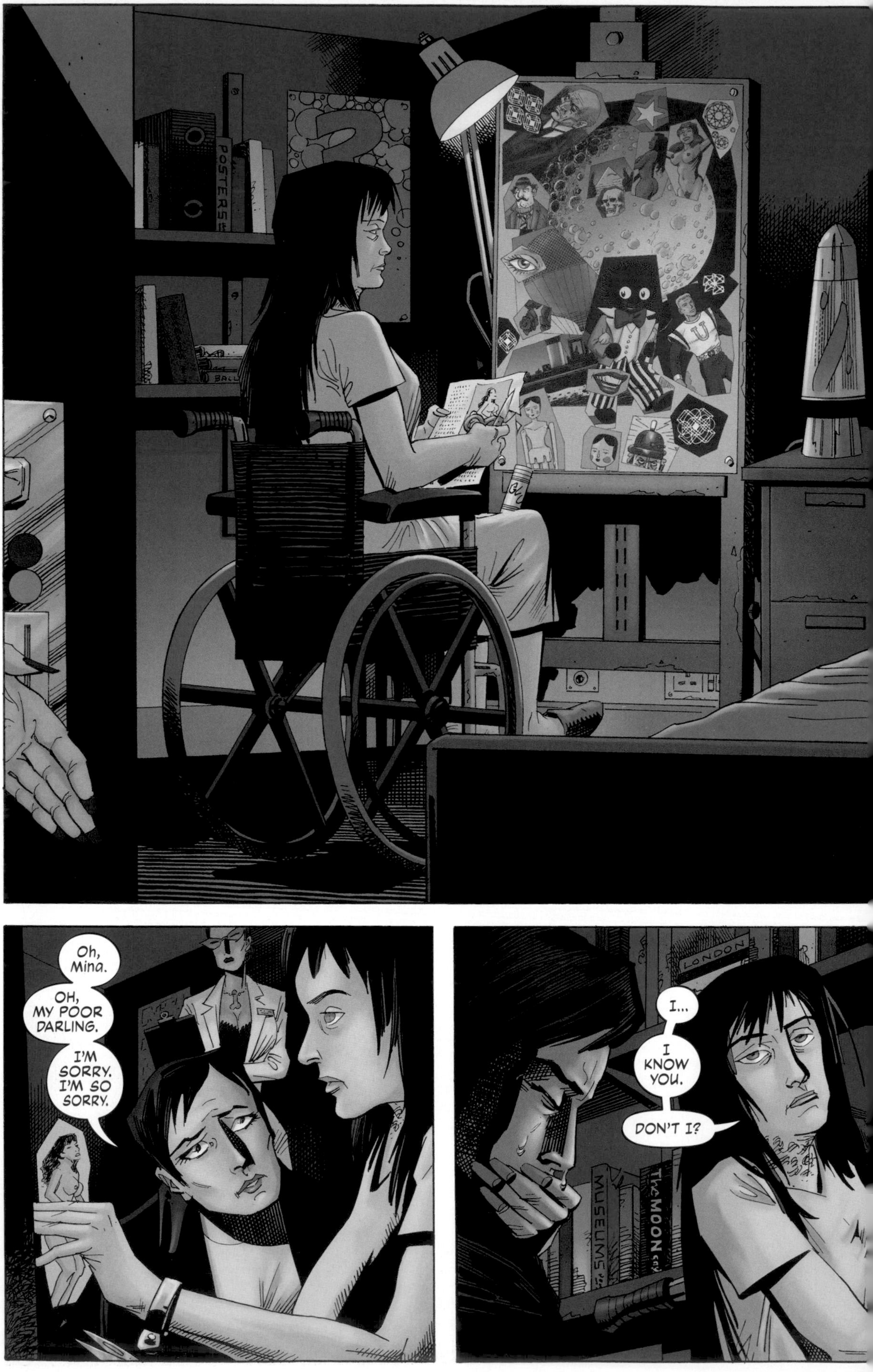
POSTERS
Oh, Mina.
OH, MY POOR DARLING.
I'M SORRY. I'M SO SORRY.
LONDON
I...
I KNOW YOU.
DON'T I?
MUSEUMS
The MOON

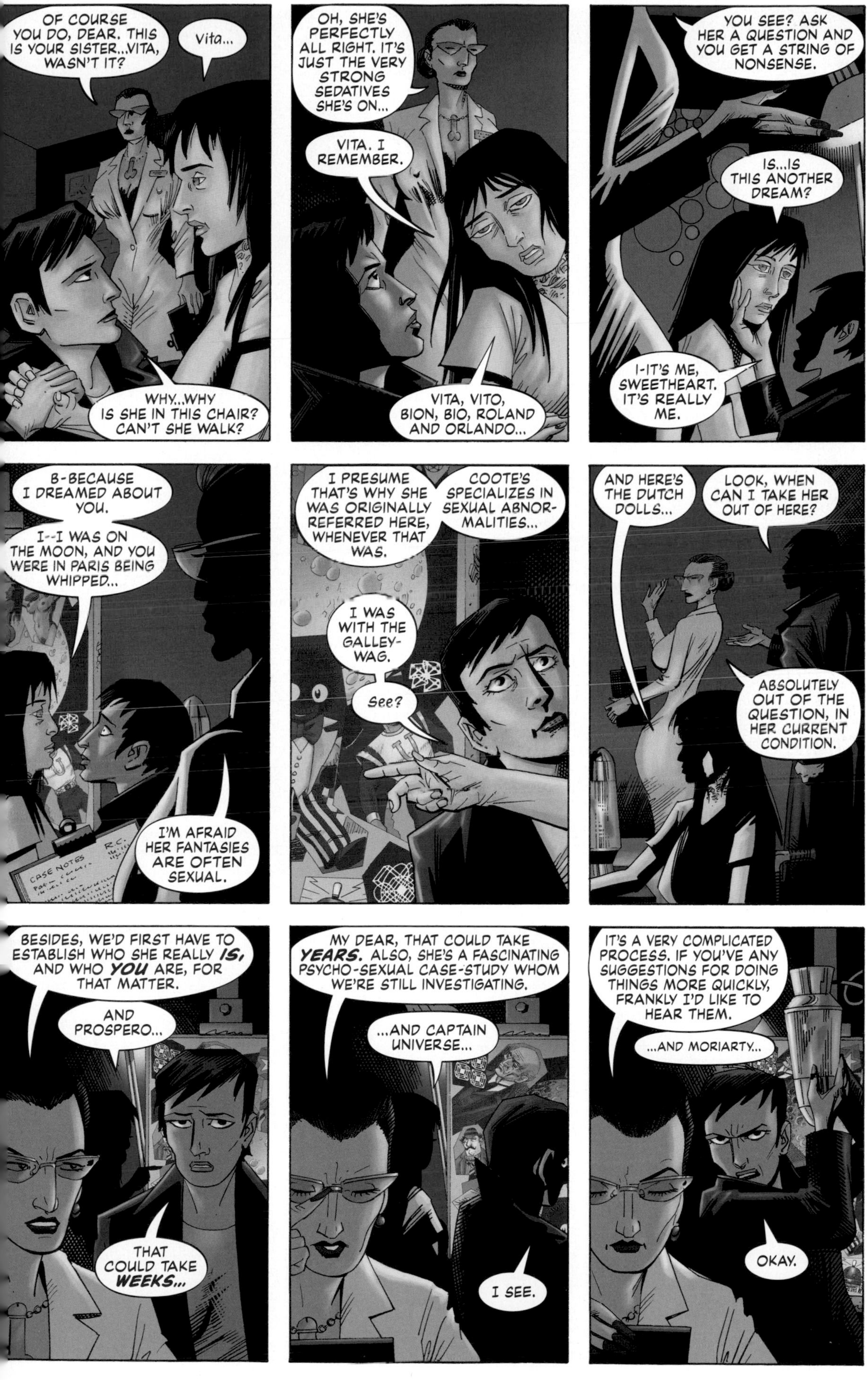
OF COURSE YOU DO, DEAR. THIS IS YOUR SISTER...VITA, WASN'T IT?
Vita...
WHY...WHY IS SHE IN THIS CHAIR? CAN'T SHE WALK?
OH, SHE'S PERFECTLY ALL RIGHT. IT'S JUST THE VERY STRONG SEDATIVES SHE'S ON...
VITA. I REMEMBER.
VITA, VITO, BION, BIO, ROLAND AND ORLANDO...
YOU SEE? ASK HER A QUESTION AND YOU GET A STRING OF NONSENSE.
IS...IS THIS ANOTHER DREAM?
I-IT'S ME, SWEETHEART. IT'S REALLY ME.
B-BECAUSE I DREAMED ABOUT YOU.
I--I WAS ON THE MOON, AND YOU WERE IN PARIS BEING WHIPPED...
I'M AFRAID HER FANTASIES ARE OFTEN SEXUAL.
CASE NOTES
R.C.
I PRESUME THAT'S WHY SHE WAS ORIGINALLY REFERRED HERE, WHENEVER THAT WAS.
COOTE'S SPECIALIZES IN SEXUAL ABNOR-MALITIES...
I WAS WITH THE GALLEY-WAG.
See?
AND HERE'S THE DUTCH DOLLS...
LOOK, WHEN CAN I TAKE HER OUT OF HERE?
ABSOLUTELY OUT OF THE QUESTION, IN HER CURRENT CONDITION.
BESIDES, WE'D FIRST HAVE TO ESTABLISH WHO SHE REALLY *IS,* AND WHO *YOU* ARE, FOR THAT MATTER.
AND PROSPERO...
THAT COULD TAKE *WEEKS...*
MY DEAR, THAT COULD TAKE *YEARS.* ALSO, SHE'S A FASCINATING PSYCHO-SEXUAL CASE-STUDY WHOM WE'RE STILL INVESTIGATING.
...AND CAPTAIN UNIVERSE...
I SEE.
IT'S A VERY COMPLICATED PROCESS. IF YOU'VE ANY SUGGESTIONS FOR DOING THINGS MORE QUICKLY, FRANKLY I'D LIKE TO HEAR THEM.
...AND MORIARTY...
OKAY.

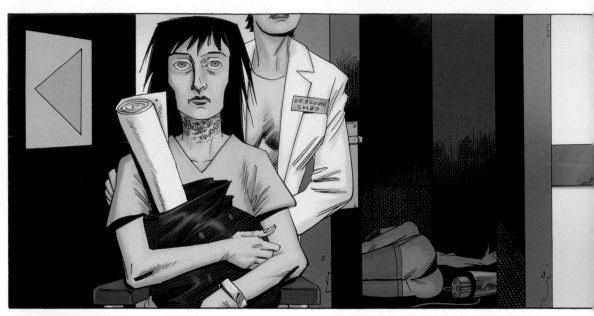

MIN IS IN BITS NOW, AL'S GONE UP IN SMOKE AND LANDO'S SEVERELY TWISTED.

BUT, TO BE FAIR, IF THEY COULDN'T TAKE A JOKE THEN THEY NEVER SHOULD HAVE BLOODY WELL ENLISTED!

THERE'S CONFLICTS LOOMING AND GUNS ARE BOOMING FROM DARFUR TO KANDAHAR.

METAL BAYONETS, THEY DON'T BEND: IT'S THE WORKER ON EACH END...

...SO IN EVERY BLITZ AND BATTLE IT'S THE COMMON FRONT-LINE CATTLE WHO IN BODY OR IN MIND GET TURNED TO PÂTÉ FOIE GRAS!

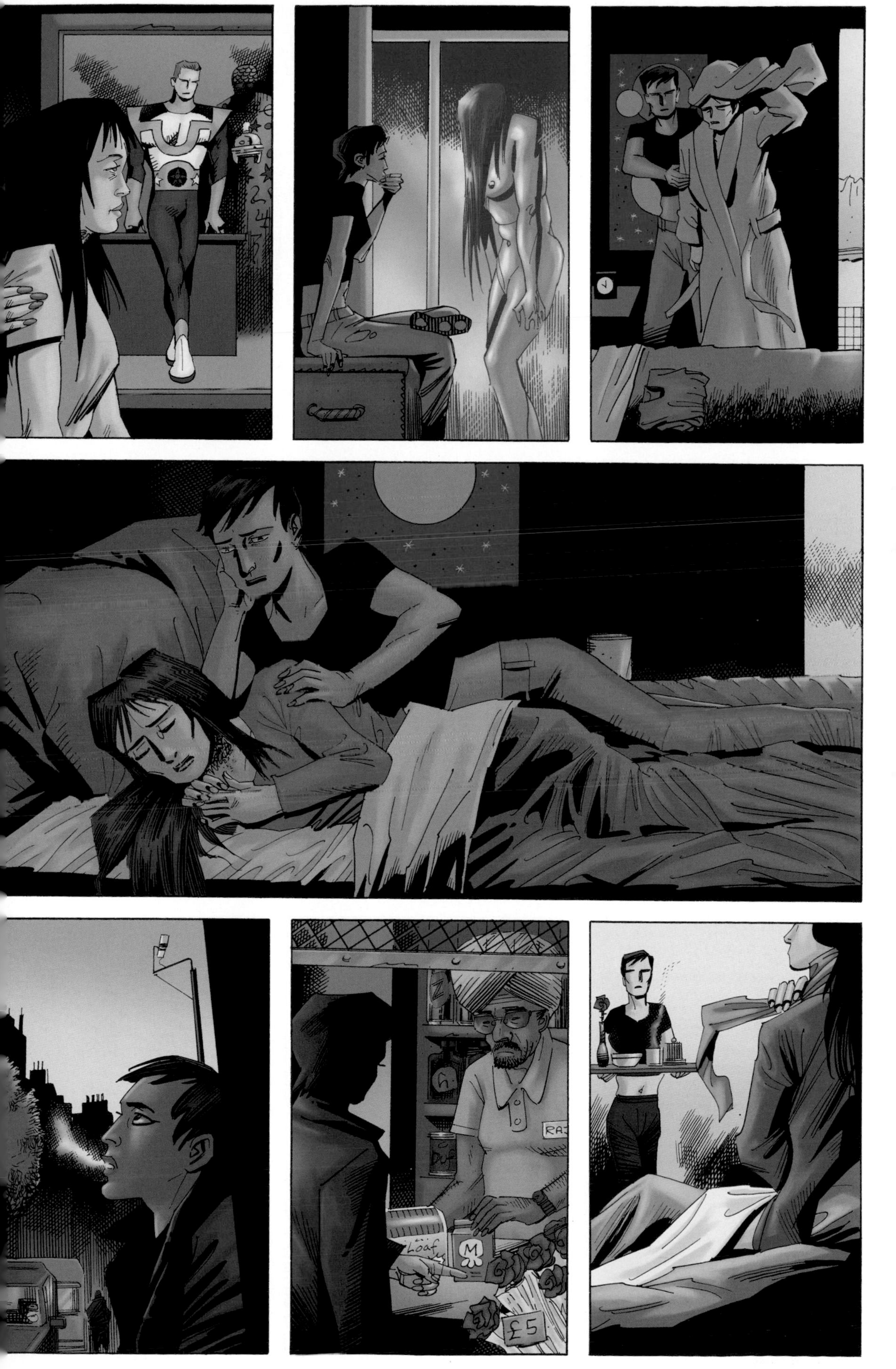
Loaf
£5

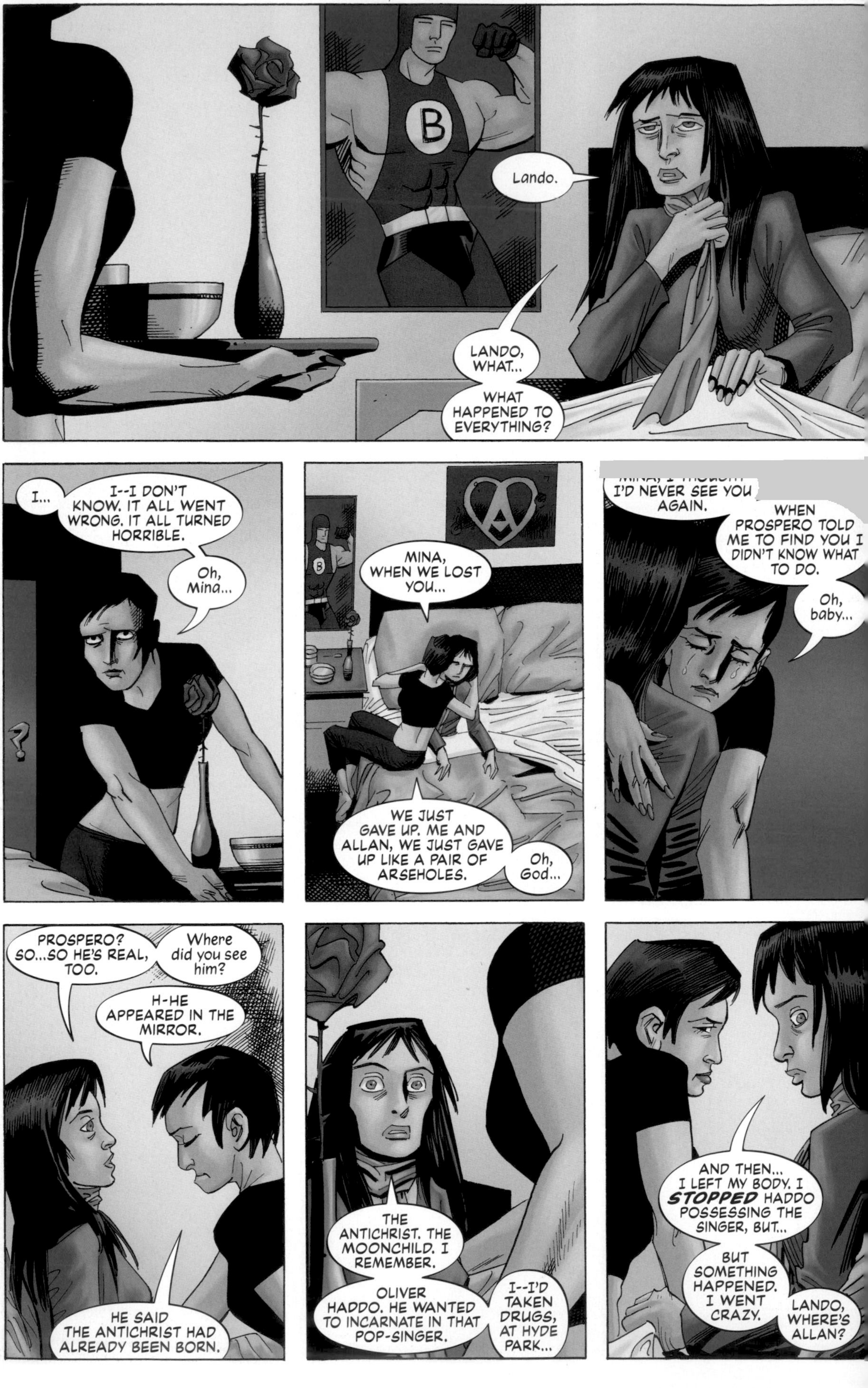
Lando.
LANDO, WHAT...
WHAT HAPPENED TO EVERYTHING?
I...
I--I DON'T KNOW. IT ALL WENT WRONG. IT ALL TURNED HORRIBLE.
Oh, Mina...
MINA, WHEN WE LOST YOU...
WE JUST GAVE UP. ME AND ALLAN, WE JUST GAVE UP LIKE A PAIR OF ARSEHOLES.
Oh, God...
I'D NEVER SEE YOU AGAIN.
WHEN PROSPERO TOLD ME TO FIND YOU I DIDN'T KNOW WHAT TO DO.
Oh, baby...
PROSPERO? SO...SO HE'S REAL, TOO.
Where did you see him?
H-HE APPEARED IN THE MIRROR.
HE SAID THE ANTICHRIST HAD ALREADY BEEN BORN.
THE ANTICHRIST. THE MOONCHILD. I REMEMBER.
OLIVER HADDO. HE WANTED TO INCARNATE IN THAT POP-SINGER.
I--I'D TAKEN DRUGS, AT HYDE PARK...
AND THEN... I LEFT MY BODY. I STOPPED HADDO POSSESSING THE SINGER, BUT...
BUT SOMETHING HAPPENED. I WENT CRAZY.
LANDO, WHERE'S ALLAN?

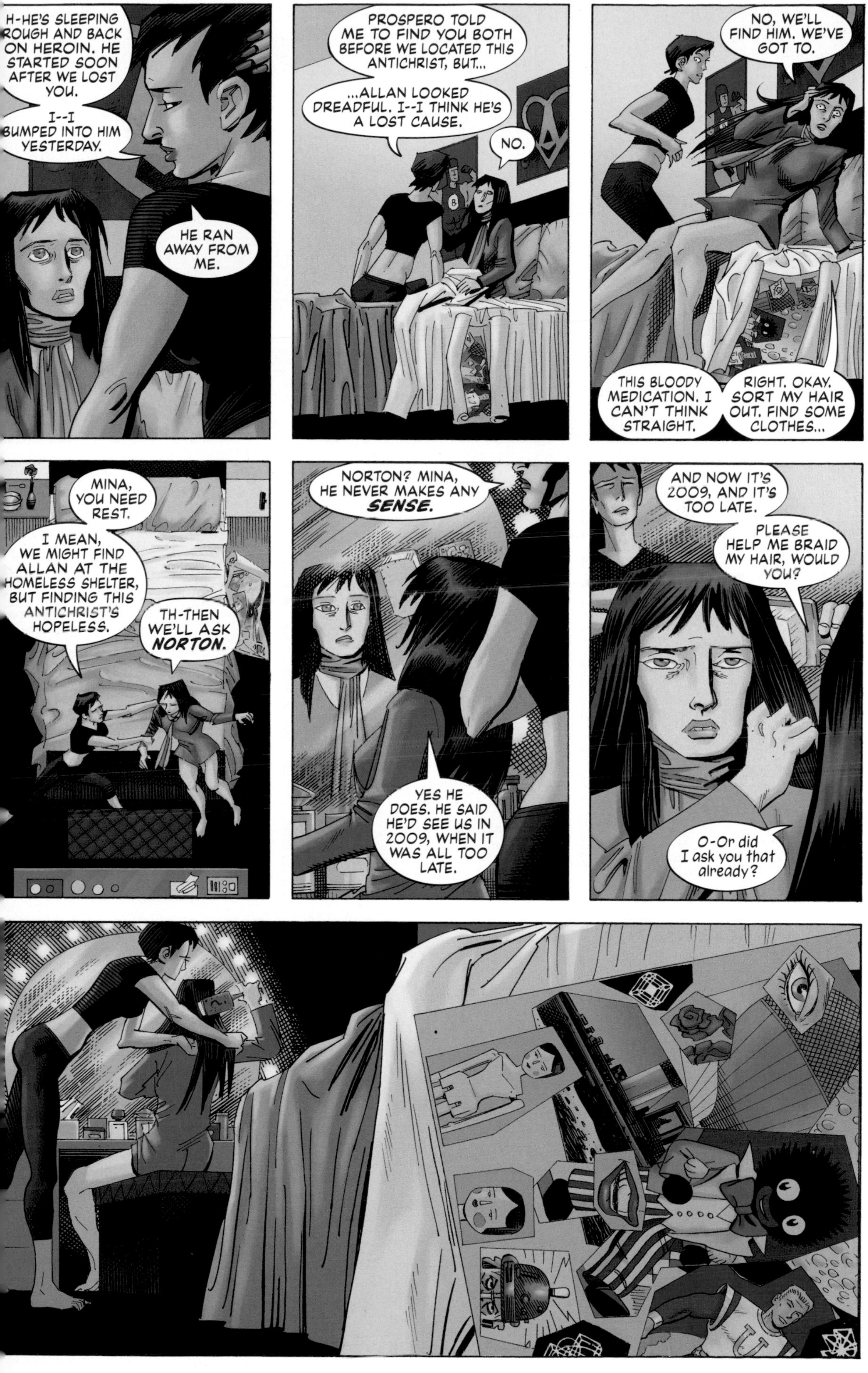
H-HE'S SLEEPING ROUGH AND BACK ON HEROIN. HE STARTED SOON AFTER WE LOST YOU.
I--I BUMPED INTO HIM YESTERDAY.
HE RAN AWAY FROM ME.
PROSPERO TOLD ME TO FIND YOU BOTH BEFORE WE LOCATED THIS ANTICHRIST, BUT...
...ALLAN LOOKED DREADFUL. I--I THINK HE'S A LOST CAUSE.
NO.
NO, WE'LL FIND HIM. WE'VE GOT TO.
THIS BLOODY MEDICATION. I CAN'T THINK STRAIGHT.
RIGHT. OKAY. SORT MY HAIR OUT. FIND SOME CLOTHES...
MINA, YOU NEED REST.
I MEAN, WE MIGHT FIND ALLAN AT THE HOMELESS SHELTER, BUT FINDING THIS ANTICHRIST'S HOPELESS.
TH-THEN WE'LL ASK NORTON.
NORTON? MINA, HE NEVER MAKES ANY SENSE.
YES HE DOES. HE SAID HE'D SEE US IN 2009, WHEN IT WAS ALL TOO LATE.
AND NOW IT'S 2009, AND IT'S TOO LATE.
PLEASE HELP ME BRAID MY HAIR, WOULD YOU?
O-Or did I ask you that already?

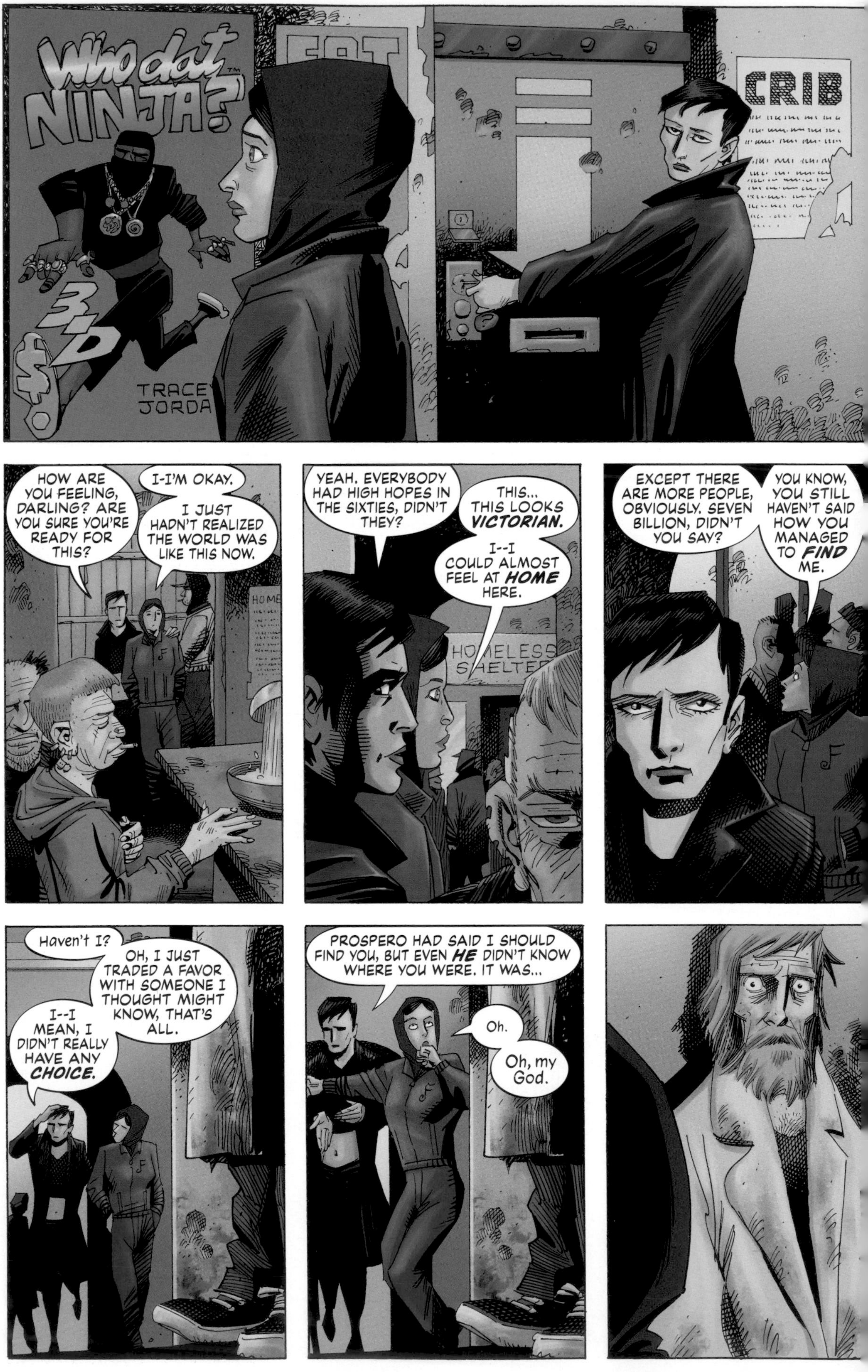
Who dat NINJA?™
3-D
$
TRACE
JORDA
CRIB
HOW ARE YOU FEELING, DARLING? ARE YOU SURE YOU'RE READY FOR THIS?
I-I'M OKAY.
I JUST HADN'T REALIZED THE WORLD WAS LIKE THIS NOW.
HOME
YEAH. EVERYBODY HAD HIGH HOPES IN THE SIXTIES, DIDN'T THEY?
THIS... THIS LOOKS **VICTORIAN.**
I--I COULD ALMOST FEEL AT **HOME** HERE.
HOMELESS SHELTER
EXCEPT THERE ARE MORE PEOPLE, OBVIOUSLY. SEVEN BILLION, DIDN'T YOU SAY?
YOU KNOW, YOU STILL HAVEN'T SAID HOW YOU MANAGED TO **FIND** ME.
Haven't I?
OH, I JUST TRADED A FAVOR WITH SOMEONE I THOUGHT MIGHT KNOW, THAT'S ALL.
I--I MEAN, I DIDN'T REALLY HAVE ANY **CHOICE.**
PROSPERO HAD SAID I SHOULD FIND YOU, BUT EVEN **HE** DIDN'T KNOW WHERE YOU WERE. IT WAS...
Oh.
Oh, my God.

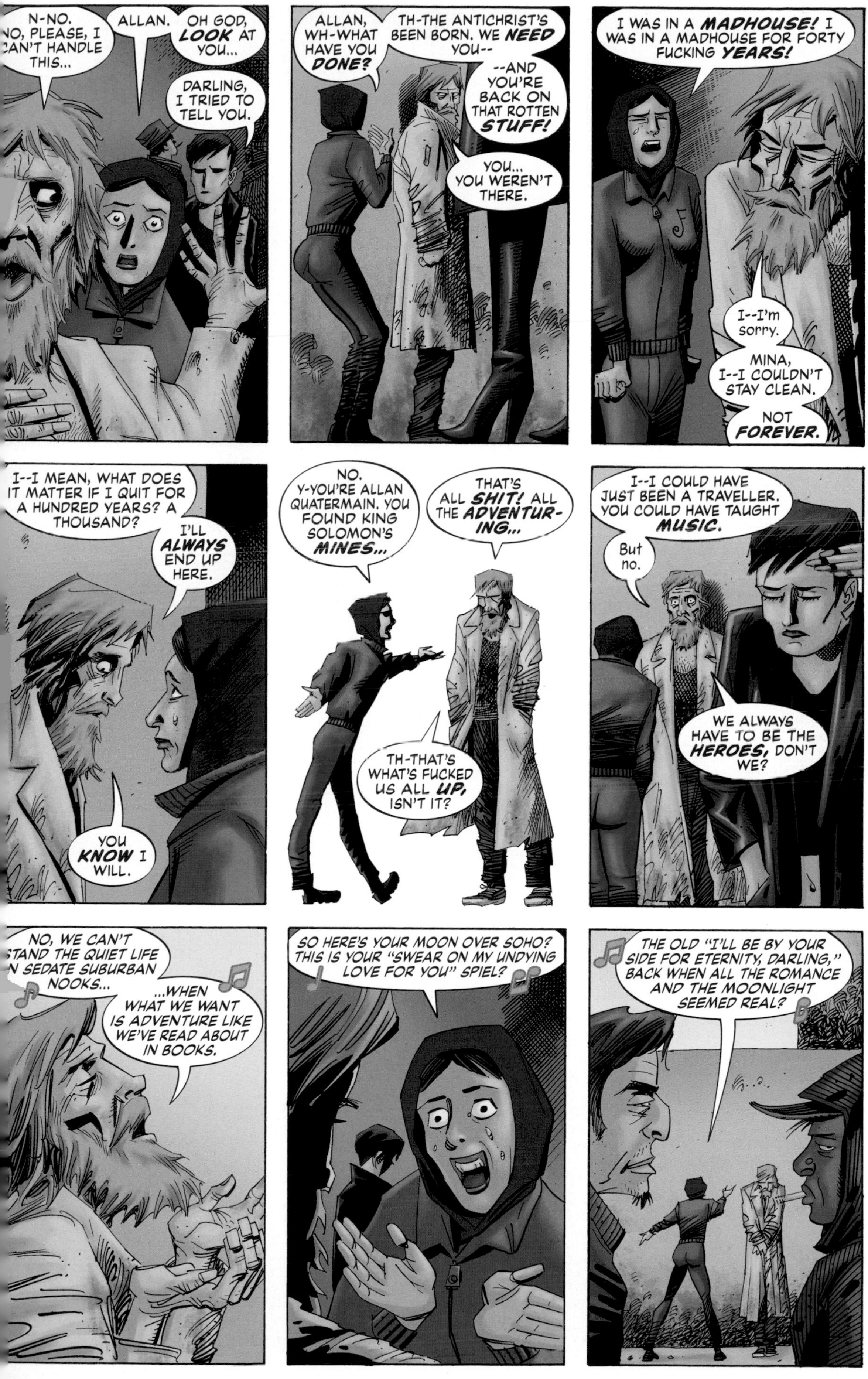
N-NO. NO, PLEASE, I CAN'T HANDLE THIS...
ALLAN.
OH GOD, LOOK AT YOU...
DARLING, I TRIED TO TELL YOU.
ALLAN, WH-WHAT HAVE YOU DONE?
TH-THE ANTICHRIST'S BEEN BORN. WE NEED YOU--
--AND YOU'RE BACK ON THAT ROTTEN STUFF!
YOU... YOU WEREN'T THERE.
I WAS IN A MADHOUSE! I WAS IN A MADHOUSE FOR FORTY FUCKING YEARS!
I--I'm sorry.
MINA, I--I COULDN'T STAY CLEAN.
NOT FOREVER.
I--I MEAN, WHAT DOES IT MATTER IF I QUIT FOR A HUNDRED YEARS? A THOUSAND?
I'LL ALWAYS END UP HERE.
YOU KNOW I WILL.
NO. Y-YOU'RE ALLAN QUATERMAIN. YOU FOUND KING SOLOMON'S MINES...
THAT'S ALL SHIT! ALL THE ADVENTURING...
TH-THAT'S WHAT'S FUCKED US ALL UP, ISN'T IT?
I--I COULD HAVE JUST BEEN A TRAVELLER. YOU COULD HAVE TAUGHT MUSIC.
But no.
WE ALWAYS HAVE TO BE THE HEROES, DON'T WE?
NO, WE CAN'T STAND THE QUIET LIFE IN SEDATE SUBURBAN NOOKS...
...WHEN WHAT WE WANT IS ADVENTURE LIKE WE'VE READ ABOUT IN BOOKS.
SO HERE'S YOUR MOON OVER SOHO? THIS IS YOUR "SWEAR ON MY UNDYING LOVE FOR YOU" SPIEL?
THE OLD "I'LL BE BY YOUR SIDE FOR ETERNITY, DARLING," BACK WHEN ALL THE ROMANCE AND THE MOONLIGHT SEEMED REAL?

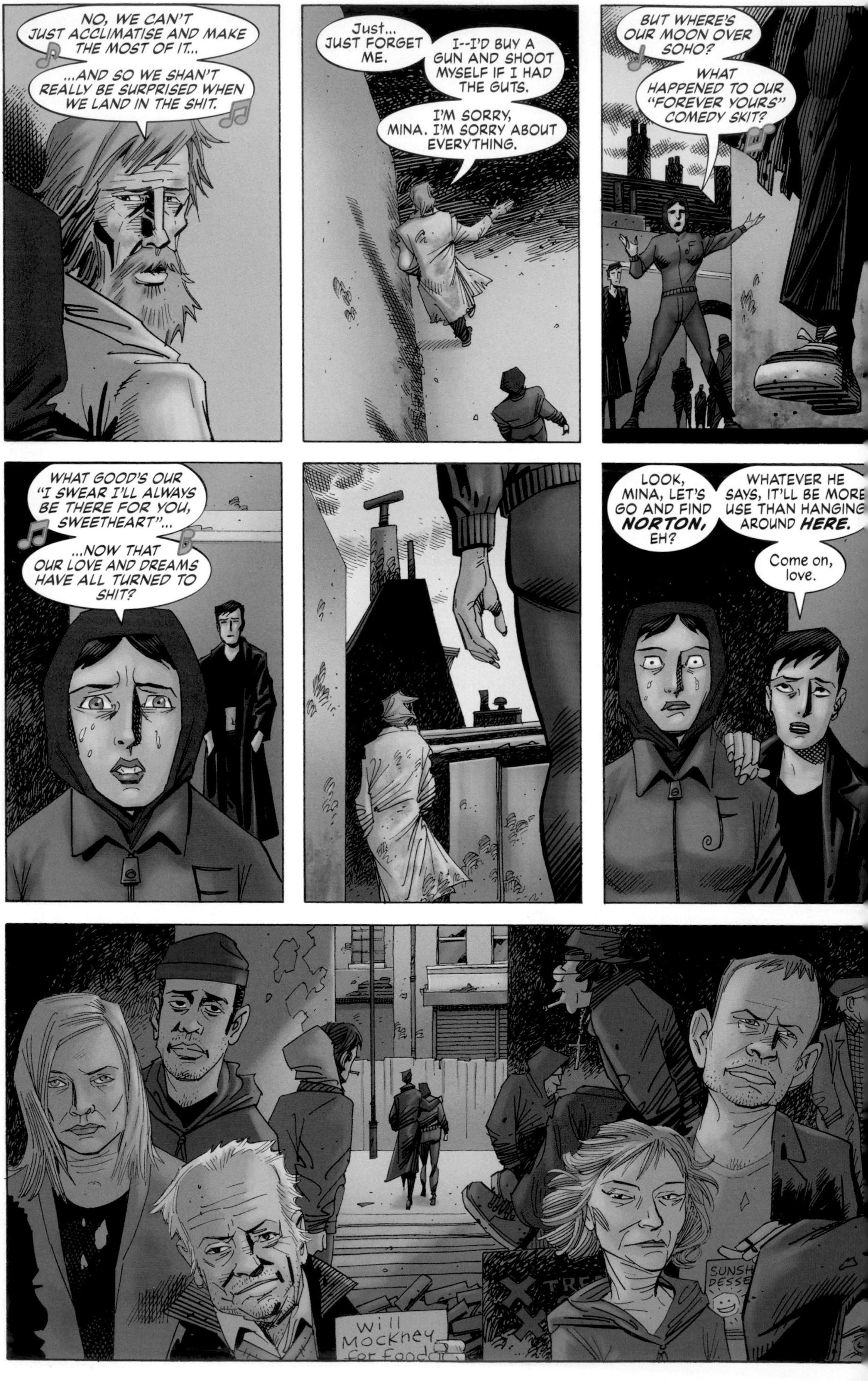
NO, WE CAN'T JUST ACCLIMATISE AND MAKE THE MOST OF IT...
...AND SO WE SHAN'T REALLY BE SURPRISED WHEN WE LAND IN THE SHIT.
Just... JUST FORGET ME.
I--I'D BUY A GUN AND SHOOT MYSELF IF I HAD THE GUTS.
I'M SORRY, MINA. I'M SORRY ABOUT EVERYTHING.
BUT WHERE'S OUR MOON OVER SOHO?
WHAT HAPPENED TO OUR "FOREVER YOURS" COMEDY SKIT?
WHAT GOOD'S OUR "I SWEAR I'LL ALWAYS BE THERE FOR YOU, SWEETHEART"...
...NOW THAT OUR LOVE AND DREAMS HAVE ALL TURNED TO SHIT?
LOOK, MINA, LET'S GO AND FIND NORTON, EH?
WHATEVER HE SAYS, IT'LL BE MORE USE THAN HANGING AROUND HERE.
Come on, love.
Will Mockney for food

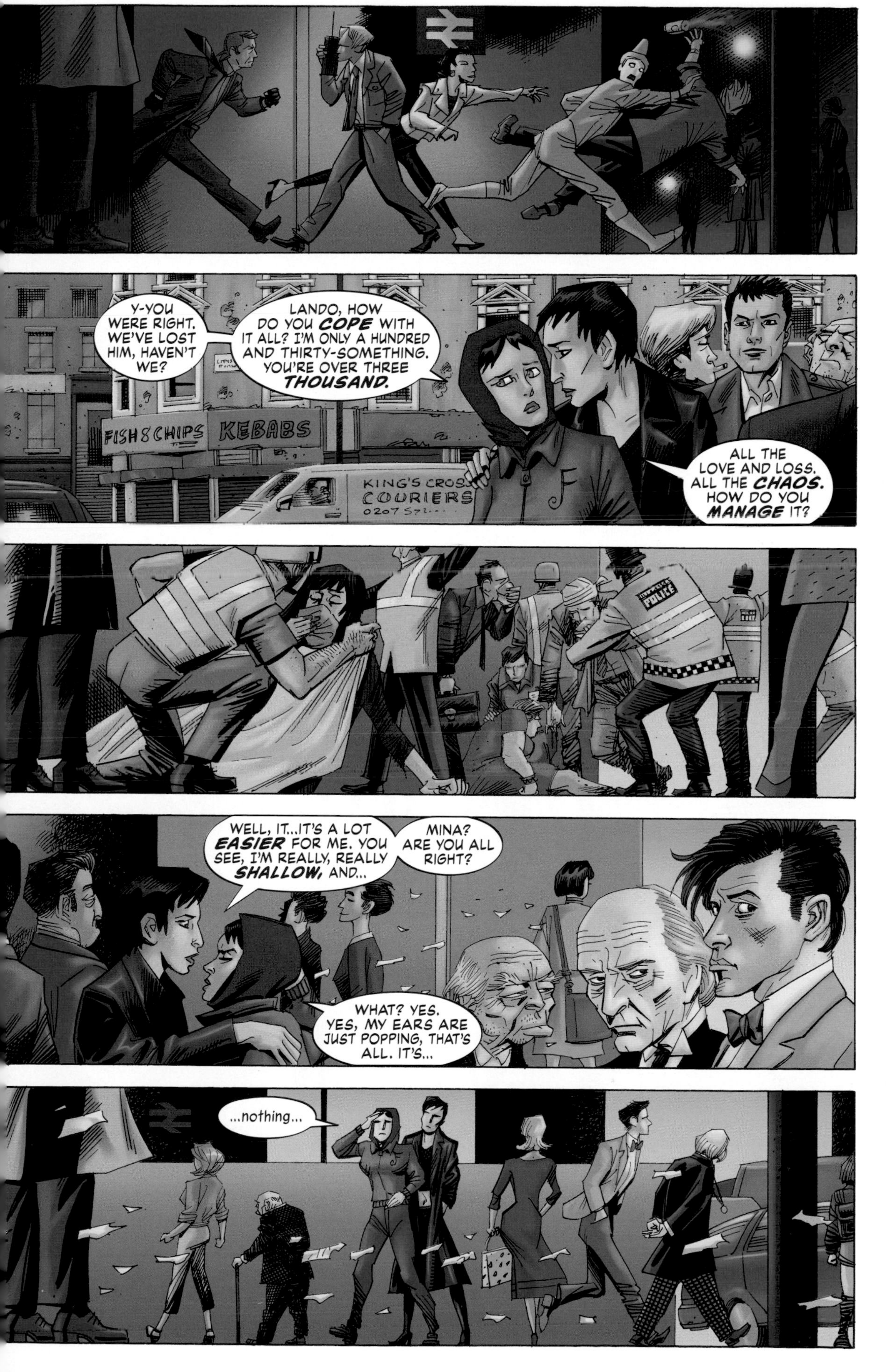

Y-YOU WERE RIGHT. WE'VE LOST HIM, HAVEN'T WE?
LANDO, HOW DO YOU COPE WITH IT ALL? I'M ONLY A HUNDRED AND THIRTY-SOMETHING. YOU'RE OVER THREE THOUSAND.
FISH & CHIPS
KEBABS
KING'S CROS
COURIERS
ALL THE LOVE AND LOSS. ALL THE CHAOS. HOW DO YOU MANAGE IT?
POLICE
WELL, IT...IT'S A LOT EASIER FOR ME. YOU SEE, I'M REALLY, REALLY SHALLOW, AND...
MINA? ARE YOU ALL RIGHT?
WHAT? YES. YES, MY EARS ARE JUST POPPING, THAT'S ALL. IT'S...
...nothing...

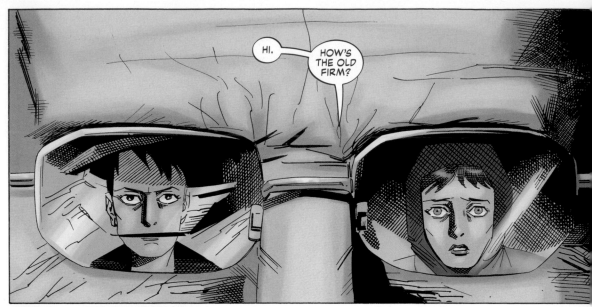

HI.

HOW'S THE OLD FIRM?

NOT... NOT SO GOOD.

HADDO'S MOONCHILD'S BEEN BORN, AND... WELL, THERE'S NOT MUCH LEFT OF US.

IT'S TOO LATE. JUST LIKE YOU SAID.

I'M SORRY TO HEAR THAT.

ARE YOU OKAY? SHOULD WE GET A CUP OF TEA OR ANYTHING?

NORTON, WE NEED *HELP*. *REAL* HELP.

FROM A SKELETAL NAZI DENTIST HAUNTING KING'S CROSS, SPOUTING VERBLESS SENTENCES? YOU MUST BE DESPERATE.

YOU'VE CERTAINLY CHANGED SINCE YOU FOUNDED LONDON HERE.

WH-WHAT?

YOU REMEMBER: GEOFFREY OF MONMOUTH'S CONFECTED ENGLISH HERITAGE. BRUTUS AT KING'S CROSS, NAMING THE CITY...

...TROY NOVANTUM.

I-IT HAPPENED *HERE*, DIDN'T IT? I'D *FOR-GOTTEN*...

A-AND AWAY FROM THE CEREMONY, I REMEMBER A MAN.

HE HAD LENSES OVER HIS EYES.

THAT WAS *YOU*.

WELL, LONDON'S FICTION *GERMINATES* HERE...

...AND IT'S HERE, IN AIDAN DUN'S *VALE ROYAL*, THAT IT FINDS ITS GROUND ZERO.

YOU MENTIONED HADDO'S MAGICAL CHILD.

LET'S GO INSIDE, SHALL WE?

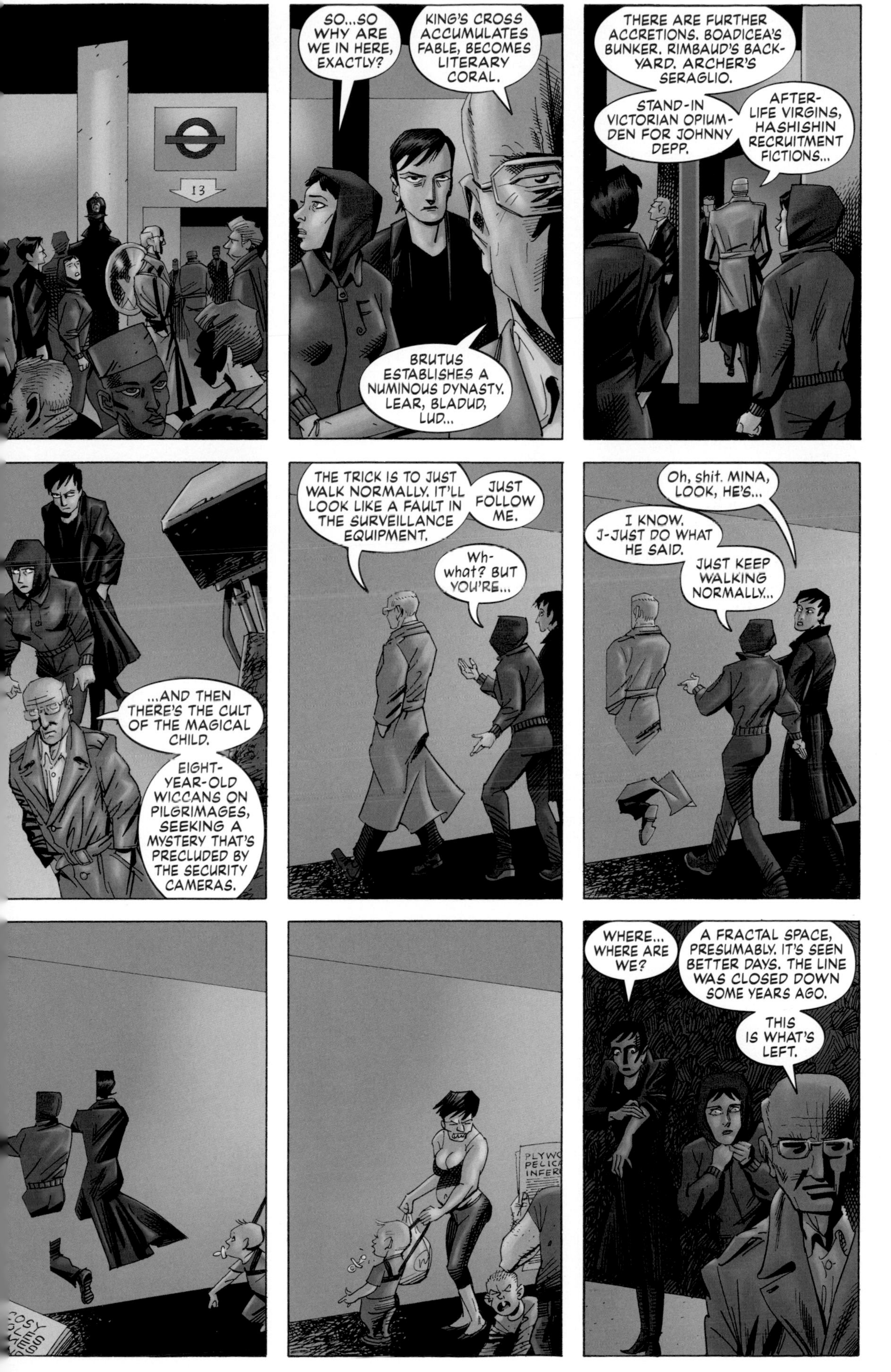
13
SO...SO WHY ARE WE IN HERE, EXACTLY?
KING'S CROSS ACCUMULATES FABLE, BECOMES LITERARY CORAL.
BRUTUS ESTABLISHES A NUMINOUS DYNASTY. LEAR, BLADUD, LUD...
THERE ARE FURTHER ACCRETIONS. BOADICEA'S BUNKER. RIMBAUD'S BACK-YARD. ARCHER'S SERAGLIO.
STAND-IN VICTORIAN OPIUM-DEN FOR JOHNNY DEPP.
AFTER-LIFE VIRGINS, HASHISHIN RECRUITMENT FICTIONS...
...AND THEN THERE'S THE CULT OF THE MAGICAL CHILD.
EIGHT-YEAR-OLD WICCANS ON PILGRIMAGES, SEEKING A MYSTERY THAT'S PRECLUDED BY THE SECURITY CAMERAS.
THE TRICK IS TO JUST WALK NORMALLY. IT'LL LOOK LIKE A FAULT IN THE SURVEILLANCE EQUIPMENT.
JUST FOLLOW ME.
Wh-what? BUT YOU'RE...
Oh, shit. MINA, LOOK, HE'S...
I KNOW. J-JUST DO WHAT HE SAID.
JUST KEEP WALKING NORMALLY...
WHERE... WHERE ARE WE?
A FRACTAL SPACE, PRESUMABLY. IT'S SEEN BETTER DAYS. THE LINE WAS CLOSED DOWN SOME YEARS AGO.
THIS IS WHAT'S LEFT.

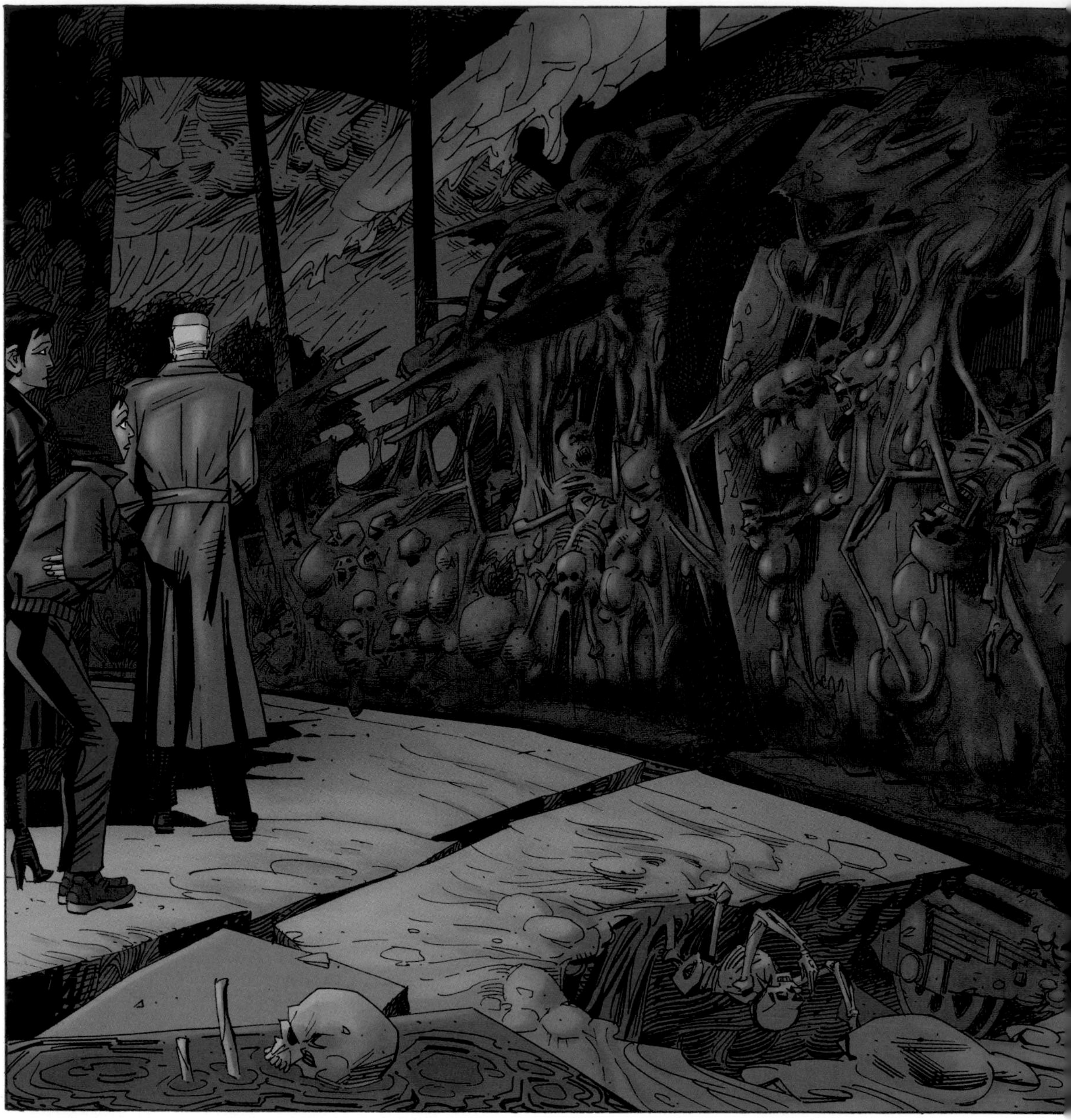

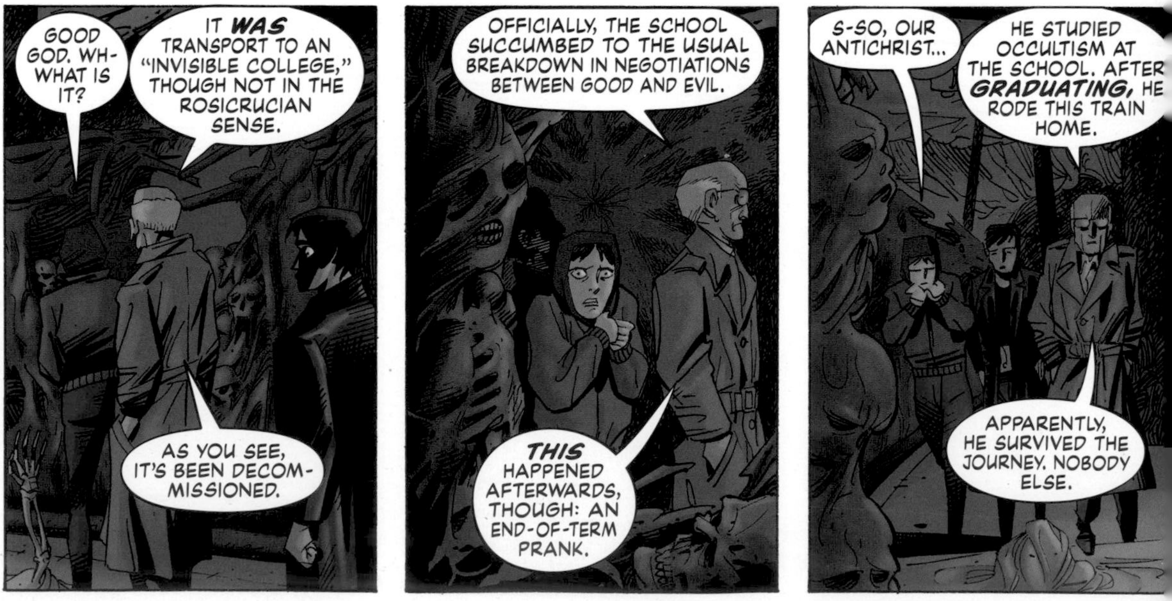
GOOD GOD. WH- WHAT IS IT?
IT WAS TRANSPORT TO AN "INVISIBLE COLLEGE," THOUGH NOT IN THE ROSICRUCIAN SENSE.
AS YOU SEE, IT'S BEEN DECOM-MISSIONED.
OFFICIALLY, THE SCHOOL SUCCUMBED TO THE USUAL BREAKDOWN IN NEGOTIATIONS BETWEEN GOOD AND EVIL.
THIS HAPPENED AFTERWARDS, THOUGH: AN END-OF-TERM PRANK.
S-SO, OUR ANTICHRIST...
HE STUDIED OCCULTISM AT THE SCHOOL. AFTER GRADUATING, HE RODE THIS TRAIN HOME.
APPARENTLY, HE SURVIVED THE JOURNEY. NOBODY ELSE.

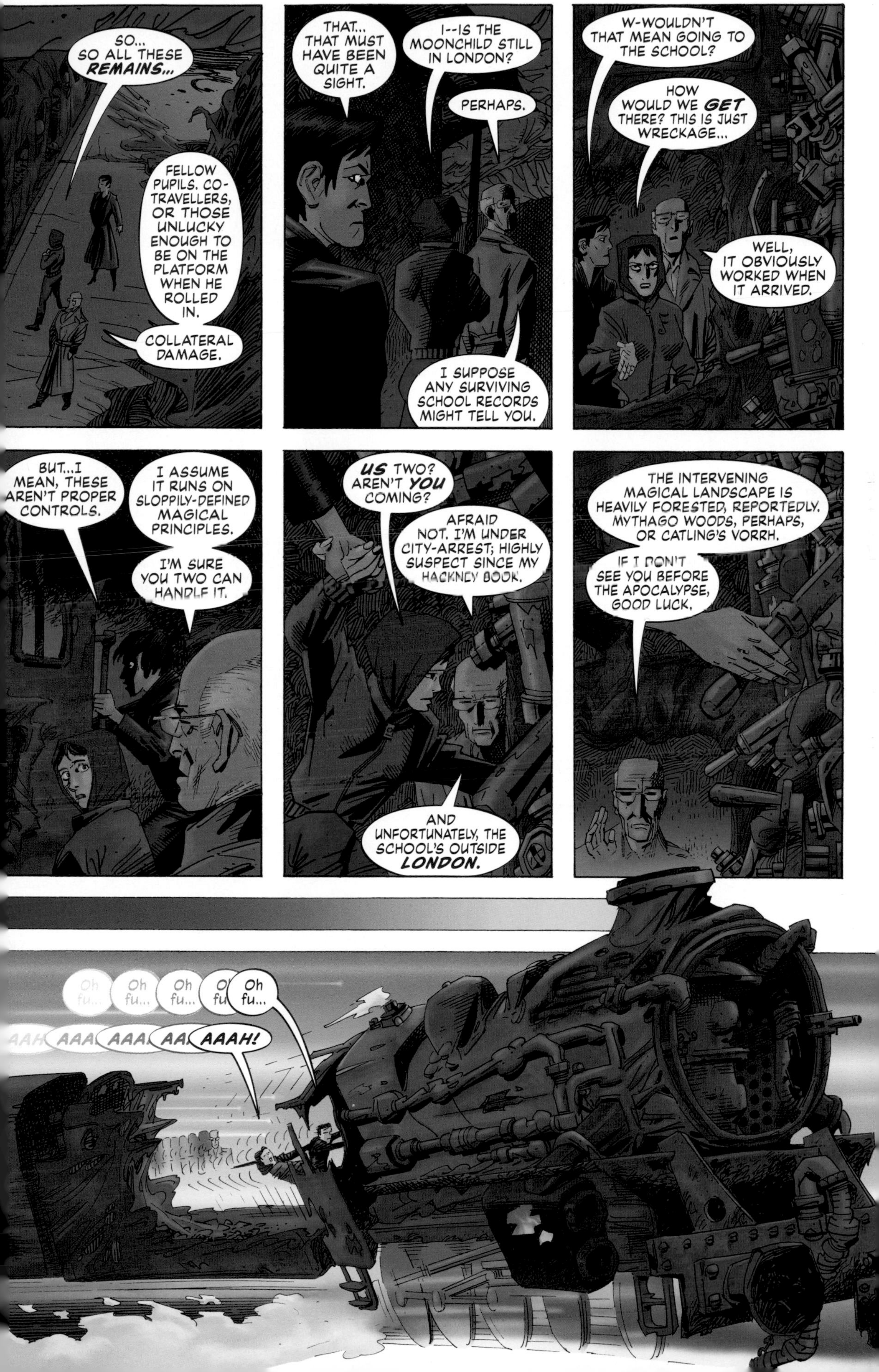
SO... SO ALL THESE REMAINS...
FELLOW PUPILS. CO-TRAVELLERS, OR THOSE UNLUCKY ENOUGH TO BE ON THE PLATFORM WHEN HE ROLLED IN.
COLLATERAL DAMAGE.
THAT... THAT MUST HAVE BEEN QUITE A SIGHT.
I--IS THE MOONCHILD STILL IN LONDON?
PERHAPS.
I SUPPOSE ANY SURVIVING SCHOOL RECORDS MIGHT TELL YOU.
W-WOULDN'T THAT MEAN GOING TO THE SCHOOL?
HOW WOULD WE GET THERE? THIS IS JUST WRECKAGE...
WELL, IT OBVIOUSLY WORKED WHEN IT ARRIVED.
BUT...I MEAN, THESE AREN'T PROPER CONTROLS.
I ASSUME IT RUNS ON SLOPPILY-DEFINED MAGICAL PRINCIPLES.
I'M SURE YOU TWO CAN HANDLE IT.
US TWO? AREN'T YOU COMING?
AFRAID NOT. I'M UNDER CITY-ARREST; HIGHLY SUSPECT SINCE MY HACKNEY BOOK.
AND UNFORTUNATELY, THE SCHOOL'S OUTSIDE LONDON.
THE INTERVENING MAGICAL LANDSCAPE IS HEAVILY FORESTED, REPORTEDLY. MYTHAGO WOODS, PERHAPS, OR CATLING'S VORRH.
IF I DON'T SEE YOU BEFORE THE APOCALYPSE, GOOD LUCK.
Oh fu...
AAAH!

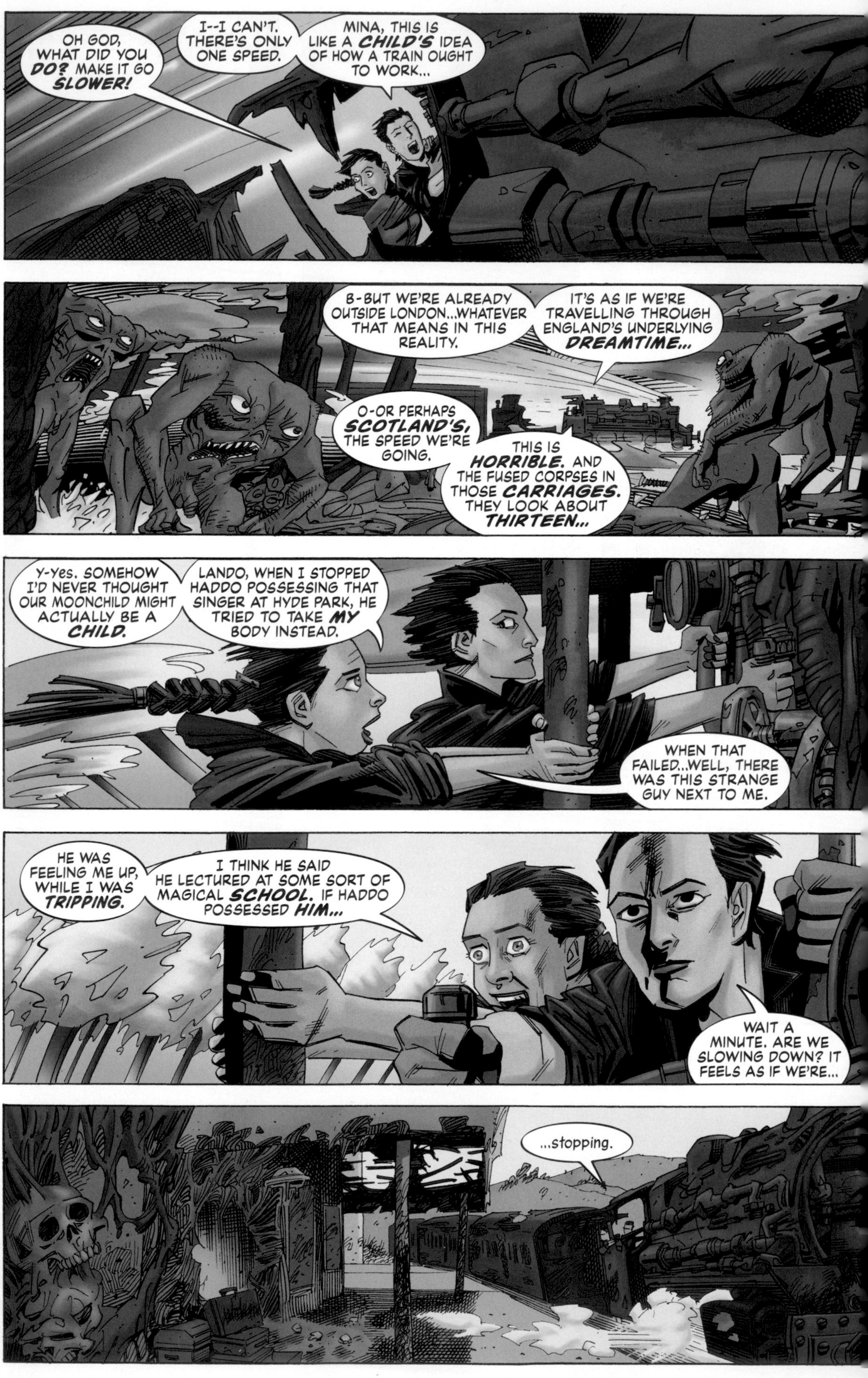

OH GOD, WHAT DID YOU DO? MAKE IT GO SLOWER!
I--I CAN'T. THERE'S ONLY ONE SPEED.
MINA, THIS IS LIKE A CHILD'S IDEA OF HOW A TRAIN OUGHT TO WORK...
B-BUT WE'RE ALREADY OUTSIDE LONDON...WHATEVER THAT MEANS IN THIS REALITY.
IT'S AS IF WE'RE TRAVELLING THROUGH ENGLAND'S UNDERLYING DREAMTIME...
O-OR PERHAPS SCOTLAND'S, THE SPEED WE'RE GOING.
THIS IS HORRIBLE. AND THE FUSED CORPSES IN THOSE CARRIAGES. THEY LOOK ABOUT THIRTEEN...
Y-Yes. SOMEHOW I'D NEVER THOUGHT OUR MOONCHILD MIGHT ACTUALLY BE A CHILD.
LANDO, WHEN I STOPPED HADDO POSSESSING THAT SINGER AT HYDE PARK, HE TRIED TO TAKE MY BODY INSTEAD.
WHEN THAT FAILED...WELL, THERE WAS THIS STRANGE GUY NEXT TO ME.
HE WAS FEELING ME UP, WHILE I WAS TRIPPING.
I THINK HE SAID HE LECTURED AT SOME SORT OF MAGICAL SCHOOL. IF HADDO POSSESSED HIM...
WAIT A MINUTE. ARE WE SLOWING DOWN? IT FEELS AS IF WE'RE...
...stopping.

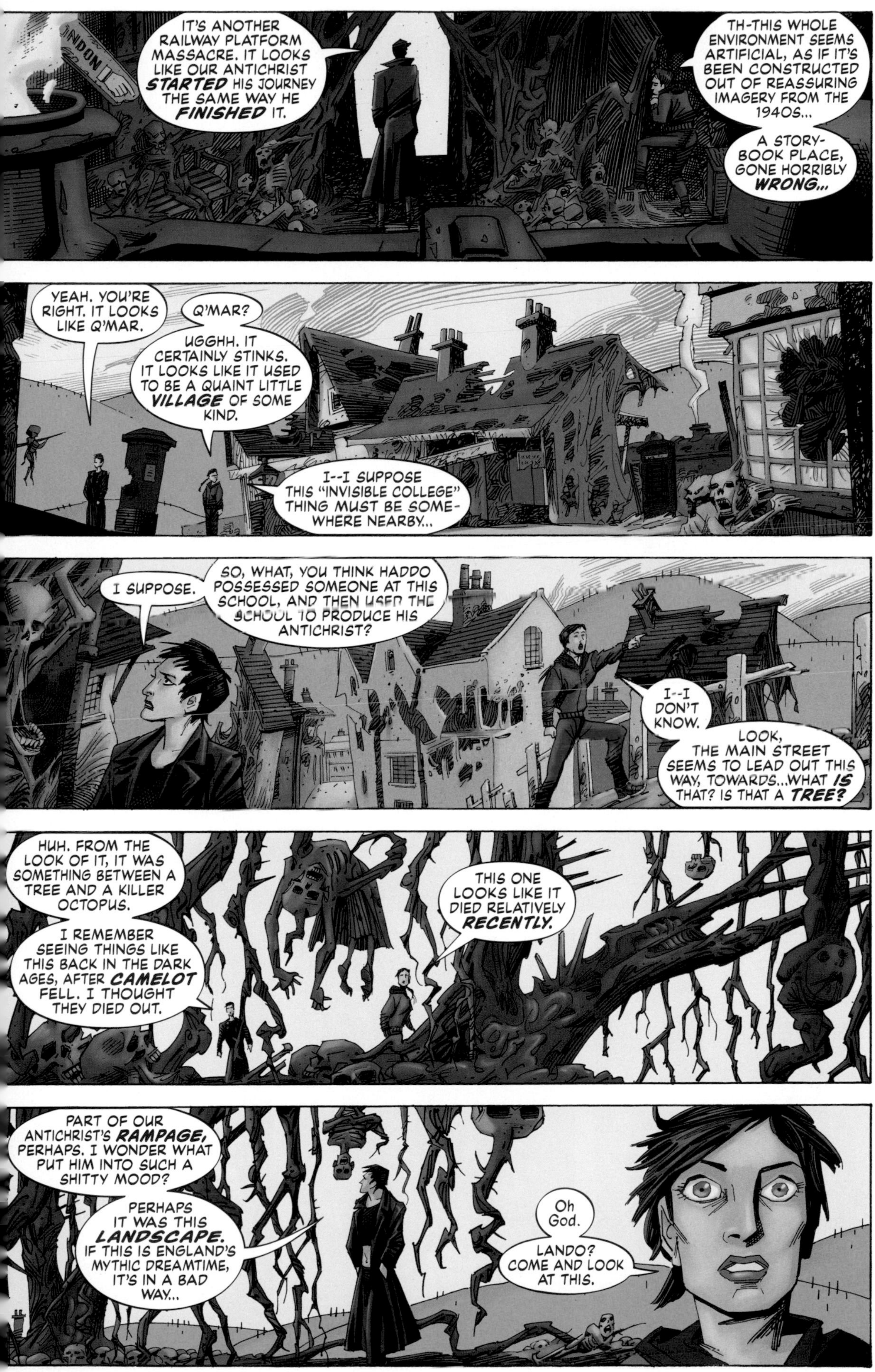

IT'S ANOTHER RAILWAY PLATFORM MASSACRE. IT LOOKS LIKE OUR ANTICHRIST STARTED HIS JOURNEY THE SAME WAY HE FINISHED IT.
TH-THIS WHOLE ENVIRONMENT SEEMS ARTIFICIAL, AS IF IT'S BEEN CONSTRUCTED OUT OF REASSURING IMAGERY FROM THE 1940S...
A STORY-BOOK PLACE, GONE HORRIBLY WRONG...
YEAH. YOU'RE RIGHT. IT LOOKS LIKE Q'MAR.
Q'MAR?
UGGHH. IT CERTAINLY STINKS. IT LOOKS LIKE IT USED TO BE A QUAINT LITTLE VILLAGE OF SOME KIND.
I--I SUPPOSE THIS "INVISIBLE COLLEGE" THING MUST BE SOME-WHERE NEARBY...
I SUPPOSE.
SO, WHAT, YOU THINK HADDO POSSESSED SOMEONE AT THIS SCHOOL, AND THEN USED THE SCHOOL TO PRODUCE HIS ANTICHRIST?
I--I DON'T KNOW.
LOOK, THE MAIN STREET SEEMS TO LEAD OUT THIS WAY, TOWARDS...WHAT IS THAT? IS THAT A TREE?
HUH. FROM THE LOOK OF IT, IT WAS SOMETHING BETWEEN A TREE AND A KILLER OCTOPUS.
I REMEMBER SEEING THINGS LIKE THIS BACK IN THE DARK AGES, AFTER CAMELOT FELL. I THOUGHT THEY DIED OUT.
THIS ONE LOOKS LIKE IT DIED RELATIVELY RECENTLY.
PART OF OUR ANTICHRIST'S RAMPAGE, PERHAPS. I WONDER WHAT PUT HIM INTO SUCH A SHITTY MOOD?
PERHAPS IT WAS THIS LANDSCAPE. IF THIS IS ENGLAND'S MYTHIC DREAMTIME, IT'S IN A BAD WAY...
Oh God.
LANDO? COME AND LOOK AT THIS.

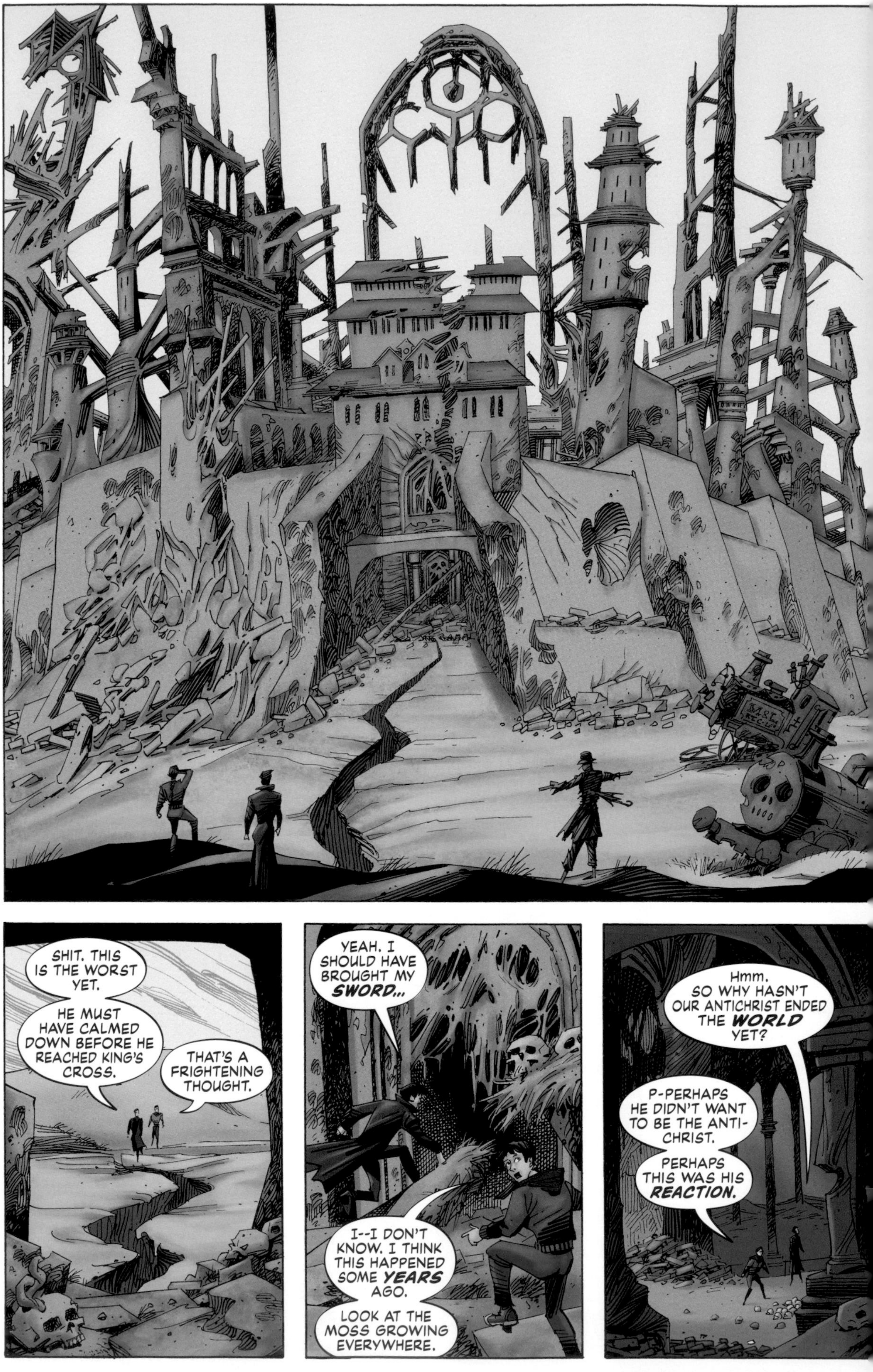
SHIT. THIS IS THE WORST YET.
HE MUST HAVE CALMED DOWN BEFORE HE REACHED KING'S CROSS.
THAT'S A FRIGHTENING THOUGHT.
YEAH. I SHOULD HAVE BROUGHT MY SWORD...
I--I DON'T KNOW. I THINK THIS HAPPENED SOME YEARS AGO.
LOOK AT THE MOSS GROWING EVERYWHERE.
Hmm. SO WHY HASN'T OUR ANTICHRIST ENDED THE WORLD YET?
P-PERHAPS HE DIDN'T WANT TO BE THE ANTI-CHRIST.
PERHAPS THIS WAS HIS REACTION.

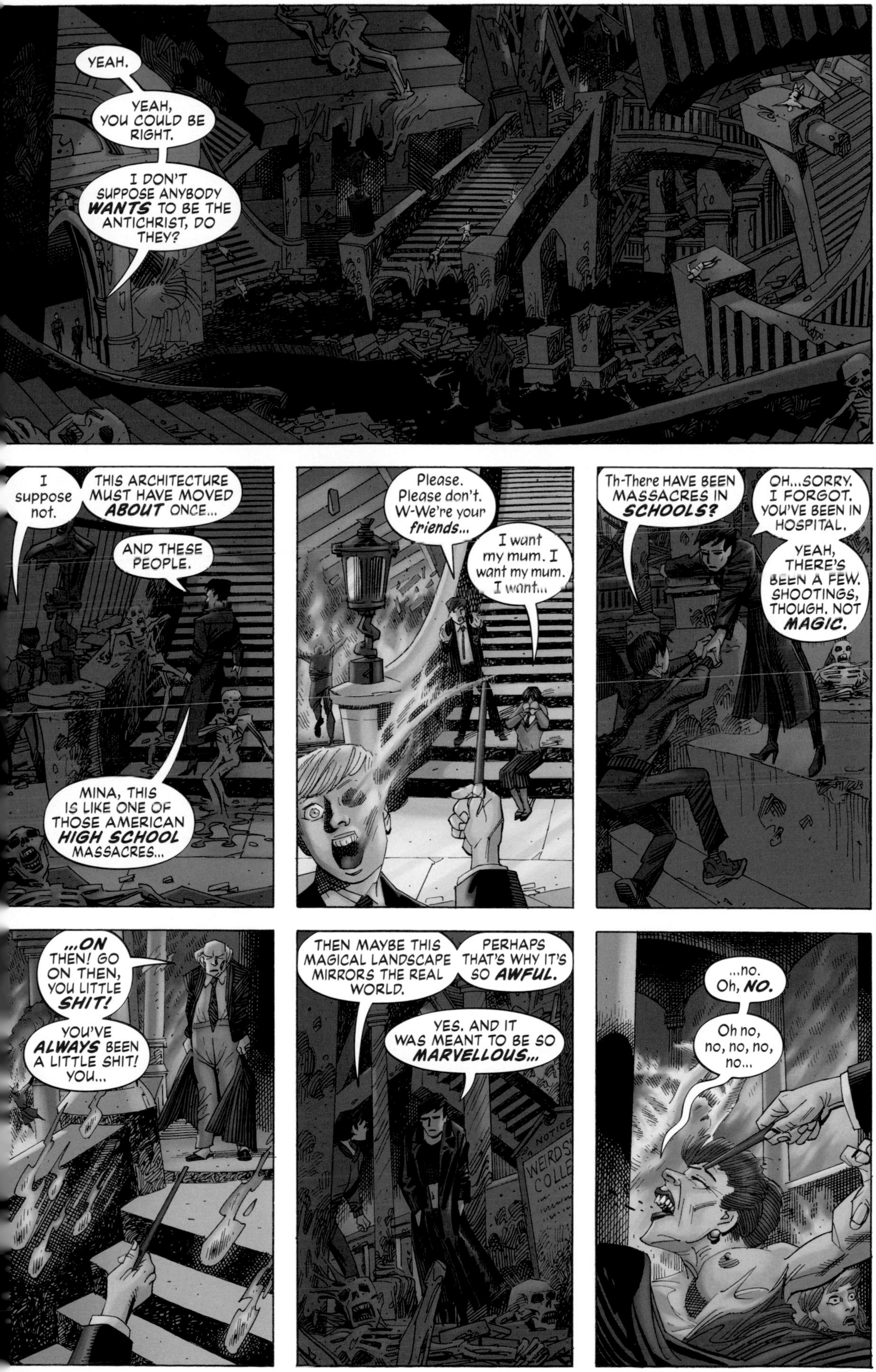
YEAH.
YEAH, YOU COULD BE RIGHT.
I DON'T SUPPOSE ANYBODY WANTS TO BE THE ANTICHRIST, DO THEY?
I suppose not.
THIS ARCHITECTURE MUST HAVE MOVED ABOUT ONCE...
AND THESE PEOPLE.
MINA, THIS IS LIKE ONE OF THOSE AMERICAN HIGH SCHOOL MASSACRES...
Please. Please don't. W-We're your friends...
I want my mum. I want my mum. I want...
Th-There HAVE BEEN MASSACRES IN SCHOOLS?
OH...SORRY. I FORGOT. YOU'VE BEEN IN HOSPITAL.
YEAH, THERE'S BEEN A FEW. SHOOTINGS, THOUGH. NOT MAGIC.
...ON THEN! GO ON THEN, YOU LITTLE SHIT!
YOU'VE ALWAYS BEEN A LITTLE SHIT! YOU...
THEN MAYBE THIS MAGICAL LANDSCAPE MIRRORS THE REAL WORLD.
PERHAPS THAT'S WHY IT'S SO AWFUL.
YES. AND IT WAS MEANT TO BE SO MARVELLOUS...
...no. Oh, NO.
Oh no, no, no, no, no...

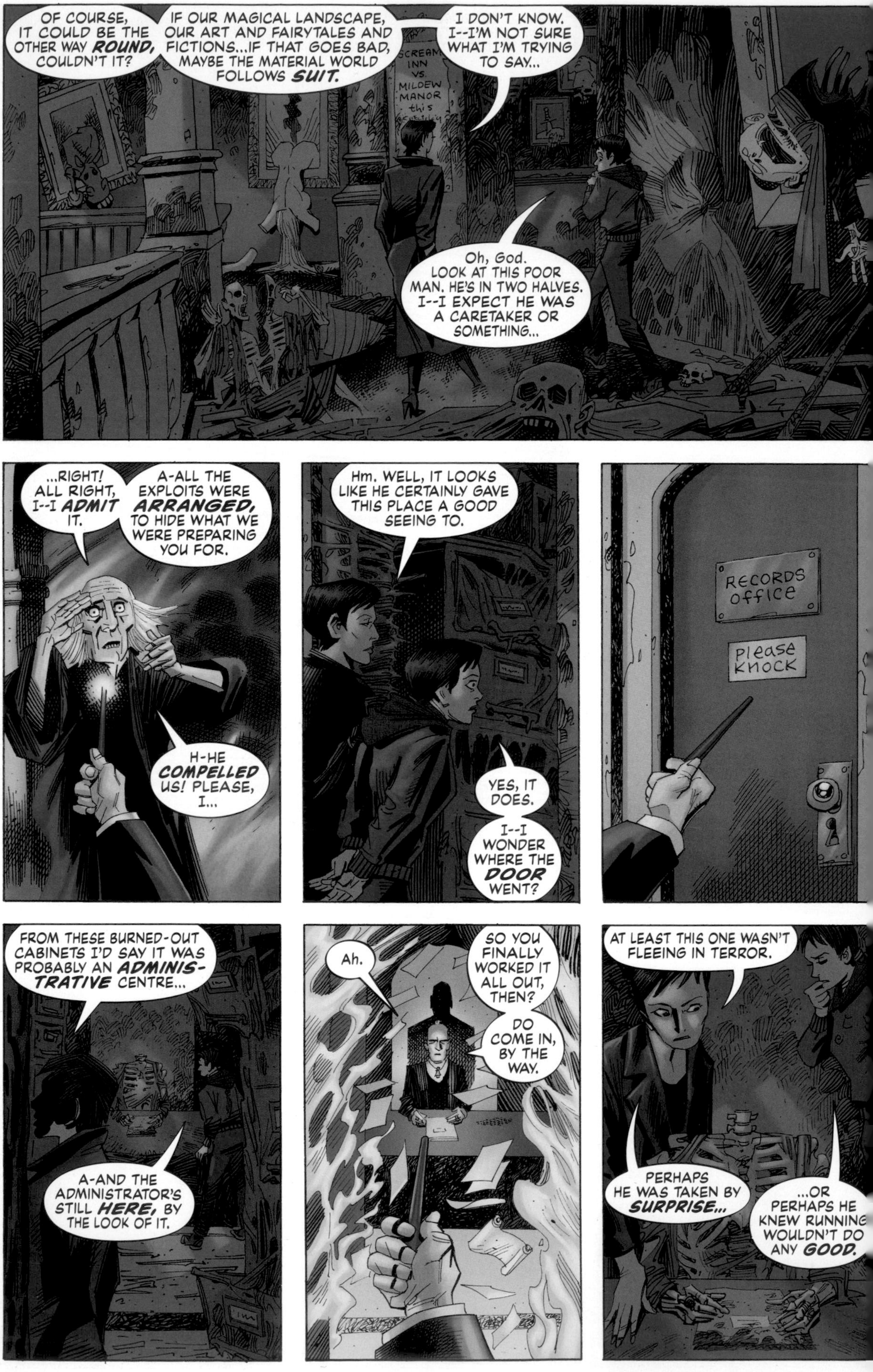
OF COURSE, IT COULD BE THE OTHER WAY ROUND, COULDN'T IT?
IF OUR MAGICAL LANDSCAPE, OUR ART AND FAIRYTALES AND FICTIONS...IF THAT GOES BAD, MAYBE THE MATERIAL WORLD FOLLOWS SUIT.
I DON'T KNOW. I--I'M NOT SURE WHAT I'M TRYING TO SAY...
SCREAM INN VS. MILDEW MANOR
Oh, God. LOOK AT THIS POOR MAN. HE'S IN TWO HALVES. I--I EXPECT HE WAS A CARETAKER OR SOMETHING...
...RIGHT! ALL RIGHT, I--I ADMIT IT.
A-ALL THE EXPLOITS WERE ARRANGED, TO HIDE WHAT WE WERE PREPARING YOU FOR.
H-HE COMPELLED US! PLEASE, I...
Hm. WELL, IT LOOKS LIKE HE CERTAINLY GAVE THIS PLACE A GOOD SEEING TO.
YES, IT DOES.
I--I WONDER WHERE THE DOOR WENT?
RECORDS office
Please knock
FROM THESE BURNED-OUT CABINETS I'D SAY IT WAS PROBABLY AN ADMINISTRATIVE CENTRE...
A-AND THE ADMINISTRATOR'S STILL HERE, BY THE LOOK OF IT.
Ah.
SO YOU FINALLY WORKED IT ALL OUT, THEN?
DO COME IN, BY THE WAY.
AT LEAST THIS ONE WASN'T FLEEING IN TERROR.
PERHAPS HE WAS TAKEN BY SURPRISE...
...OR PERHAPS HE KNEW RUNNING WOULDN'T DO ANY GOOD.

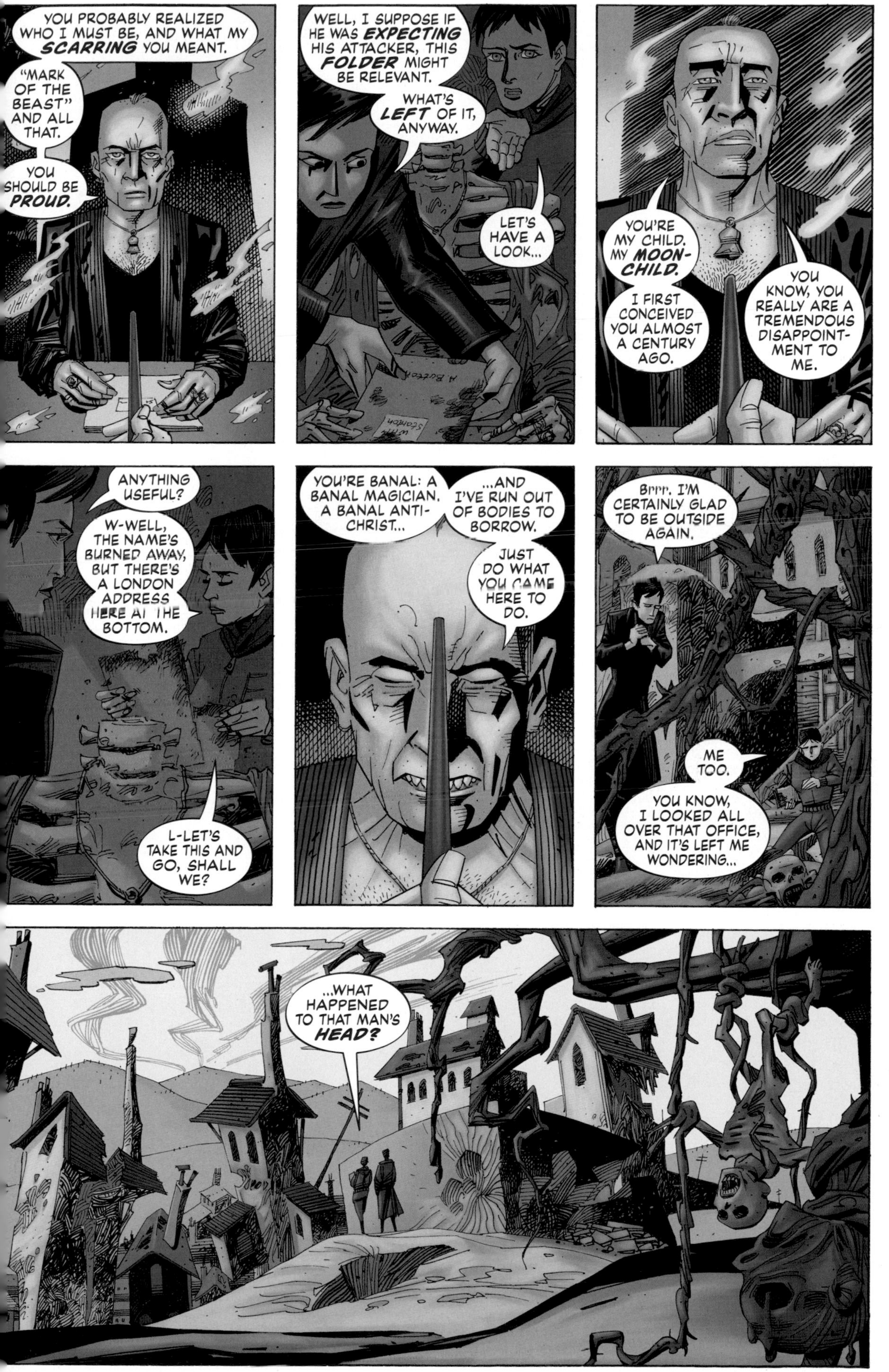
YOU PROBABLY REALIZED WHO I MUST BE, AND WHAT MY SCARRING YOU MEANT.
"MARK OF THE BEAST" AND ALL THAT.
YOU SHOULD BE PROUD.
WELL, I SUPPOSE IF HE WAS EXPECTING HIS ATTACKER, THIS FOLDER MIGHT BE RELEVANT.
WHAT'S LEFT OF IT, ANYWAY.
LET'S HAVE A LOOK...
YOU'RE MY CHILD. MY MOON-CHILD.
I FIRST CONCEIVED YOU ALMOST A CENTURY AGO.
YOU KNOW, YOU REALLY ARE A TREMENDOUS DISAPPOINT-MENT TO ME.
ANYTHING USEFUL?
W-WELL, THE NAME'S BURNED AWAY, BUT THERE'S A LONDON ADDRESS HERE AT THE BOTTOM.
L-LET'S TAKE THIS AND GO, SHALL WE?
YOU'RE BANAL: A BANAL MAGICIAN. A BANAL ANTI-CHRIST...
...AND I'VE RUN OUT OF BODIES TO BORROW.
JUST DO WHAT YOU CAME HERE TO DO.
Brrr. I'M CERTAINLY GLAD TO BE OUTSIDE AGAIN.
ME TOO.
YOU KNOW, I LOOKED ALL OVER THAT OFFICE, AND IT'S LEFT ME WONDERING...
...WHAT HAPPENED TO THAT MAN'S HEAD?

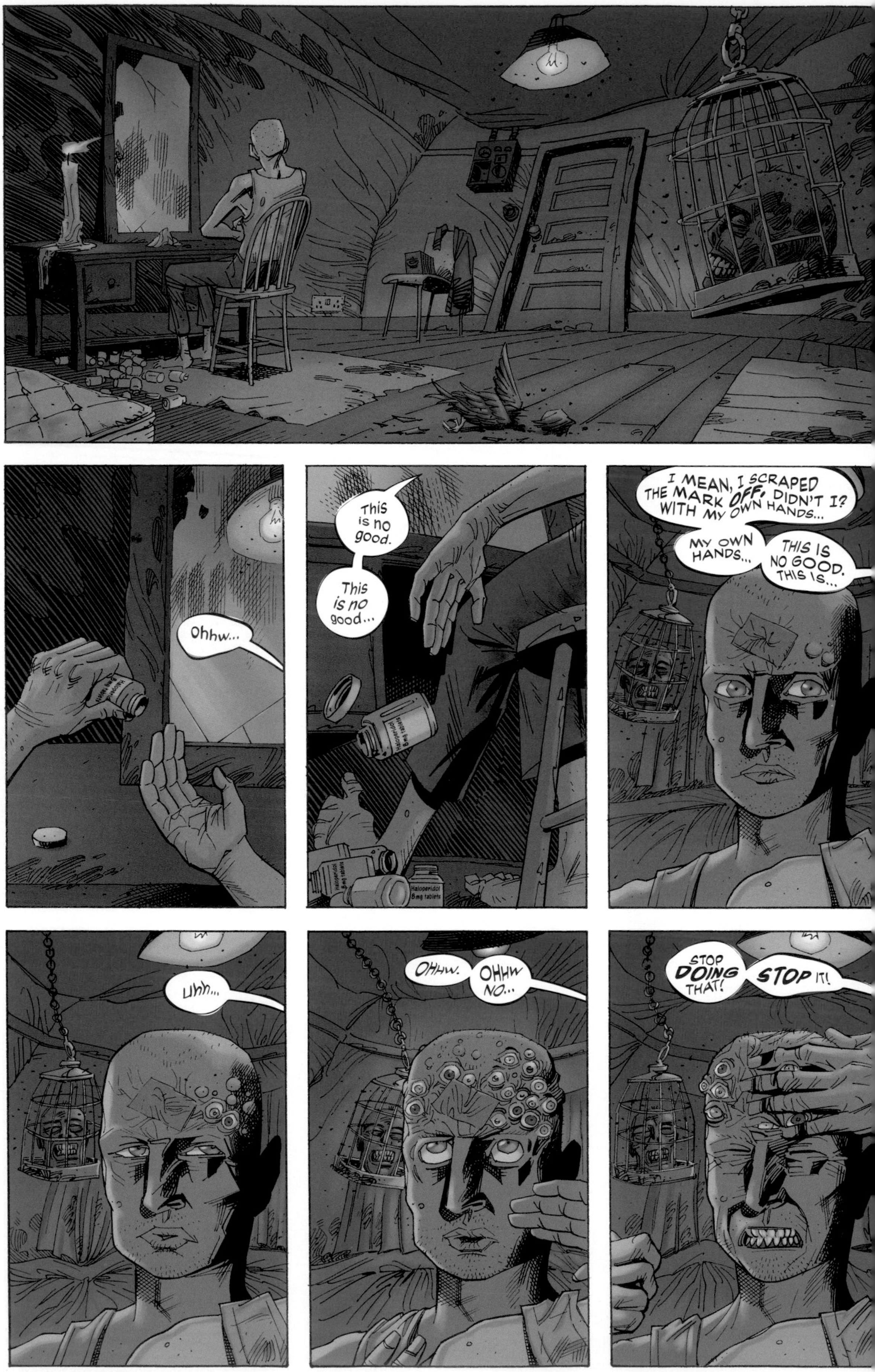
Ohhw...
This is no good.
This is no good...
Haloperidol 5mg tablets
I MEAN, I SCRAPED THE MARK OFF, DIDN'T I? WITH MY OWN HANDS...
MY OWN HANDS...
THIS IS NO GOOD. THIS IS...
Uhh...
OHHW.
OHHW NO...
STOP DOING THAT!
STOP IT!

nn...

LOOK AT ME! LOOK AT THE... ALL THE *EYES!* ALL THE...STUFF.

YOU DID THIS, YOU KNOW. I'M REALLY, REALLY *ANGRY* WITH YOU!

HOW LONG HAVE WE *BEEN* HERE, ANYWAY?

I'D PLANNED ON A FEW DAYS, BUT ALL MY *MEDICINE'S* GONE, AND...

I--IT'S BEEN *YEARS,* HASN'T IT?

YEARS AND YEARS. AND NOW I'M ALL *OLD!*

ARE YOU *HAPPY* NOW? IS THIS WHAT YOU *WANTED!* ALL THESE *FLIES* AND EVERYTHING?

IS IT?

N-No.

No, this... this isn't what I wanted.

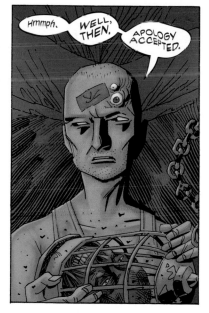

Hmmph.

WELL, THEN.

APOLOGY ACCEPTED.

WE'LL SAY NO MORE ABOUT IT.

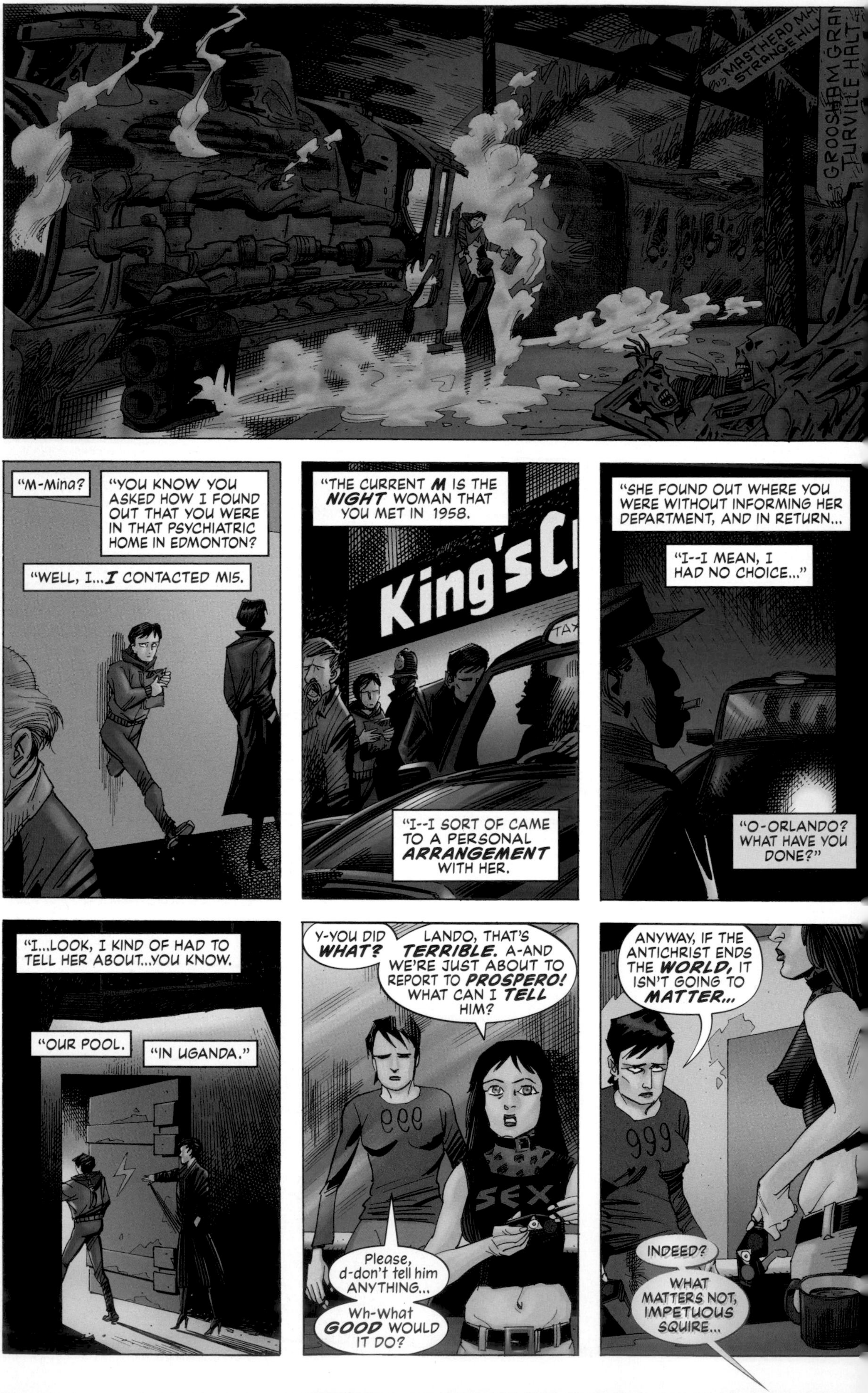
MASTHEAD MA
STRANGE HILL
GROOSHAM GRAN
TURVILLE HALT
"M-Mina?
"YOU KNOW YOU ASKED HOW I FOUND OUT THAT YOU WERE IN THAT PSYCHIATRIC HOME IN EDMONTON?
"WELL, I...I CONTACTED MI5.
"THE CURRENT M IS THE NIGHT WOMAN THAT YOU MET IN 1958.
King's C
"I--I SORT OF CAME TO A PERSONAL ARRANGEMENT WITH HER.
"SHE FOUND OUT WHERE YOU WERE WITHOUT INFORMING HER DEPARTMENT, AND IN RETURN...
"I--I MEAN, I HAD NO CHOICE..."
"O-ORLANDO? WHAT HAVE YOU DONE?"
"I...LOOK, I KIND OF HAD TO TELL HER ABOUT...YOU KNOW.
"OUR POOL.
"IN UGANDA."
Y-YOU DID WHAT?
LANDO, THAT'S TERRIBLE. A-AND WE'RE JUST ABOUT TO REPORT TO PROSPERO! WHAT CAN I TELL HIM?
Please, d-don't tell him ANYTHING...
Wh-What GOOD WOULD IT DO?
SEX
ANYWAY, IF THE ANTICHRIST ENDS THE WORLD, IT ISN'T GOING TO MATTER...
INDEED?
WHAT MATTERS NOT, IMPETUOUS SQUIRE...

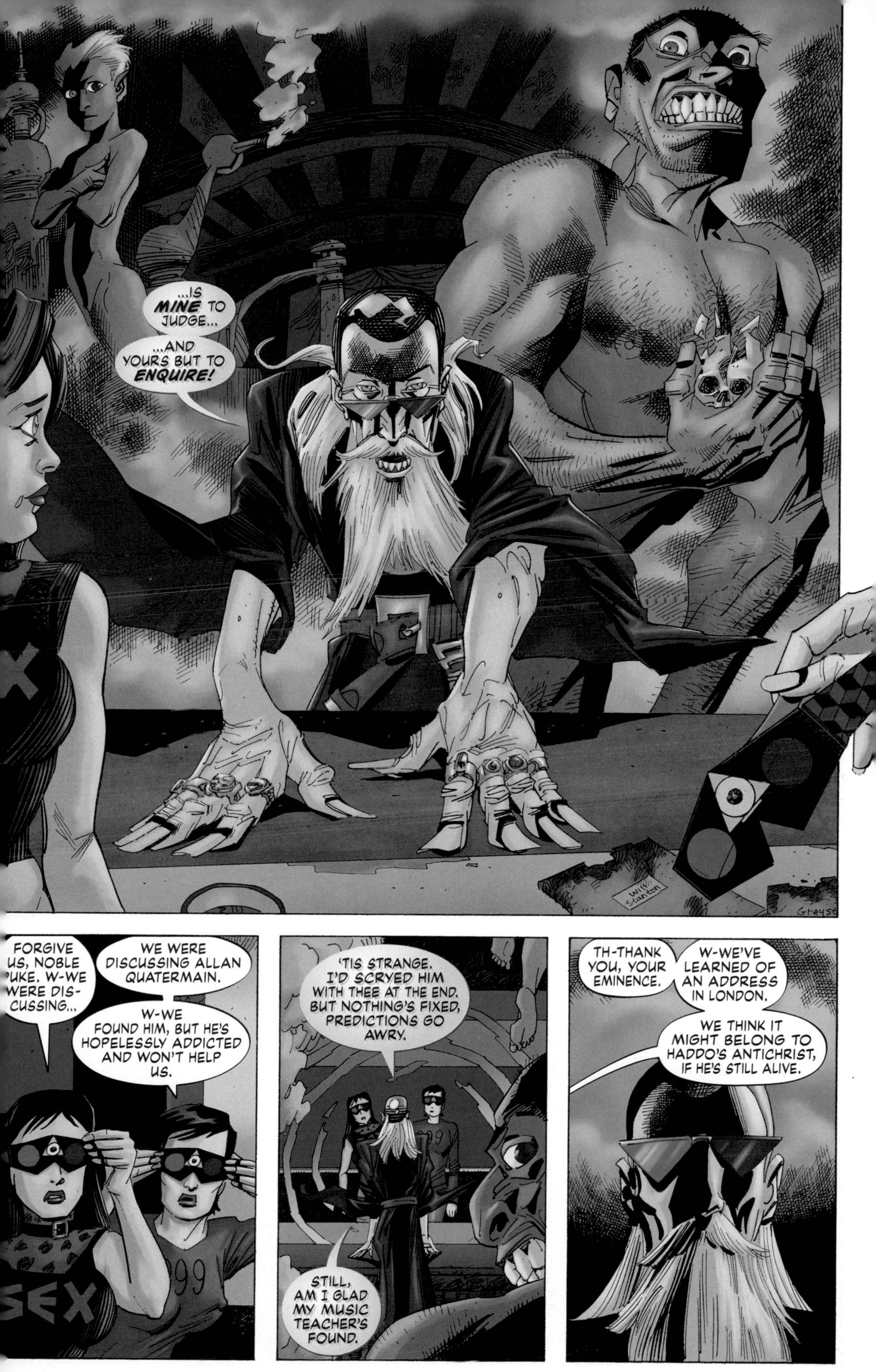
...IS MINE TO JUDGE...
...AND YOURS BUT TO ENQUIRE!
WILL STANTON
FORGIVE US, NOBLE DUKE. W-WE WERE DIS-CUSSING...
WE WERE DISCUSSING ALLAN QUATERMAIN.
W-WE FOUND HIM, BUT HE'S HOPELESSLY ADDICTED AND WON'T HELP US.
'TIS STRANGE. I'D SCRYED HIM WITH THEE AT THE END. BUT NOTHING'S FIXED, PREDICTIONS GO AWRY.
STILL, AM I GLAD MY MUSIC TEACHER'S FOUND.
TH-THANK YOU, YOUR EMINENCE.
W-WE'VE LEARNED OF AN ADDRESS IN LONDON.
WE THINK IT MIGHT BELONG TO HADDO'S ANTICHRIST, IF HE'S STILL ALIVE.

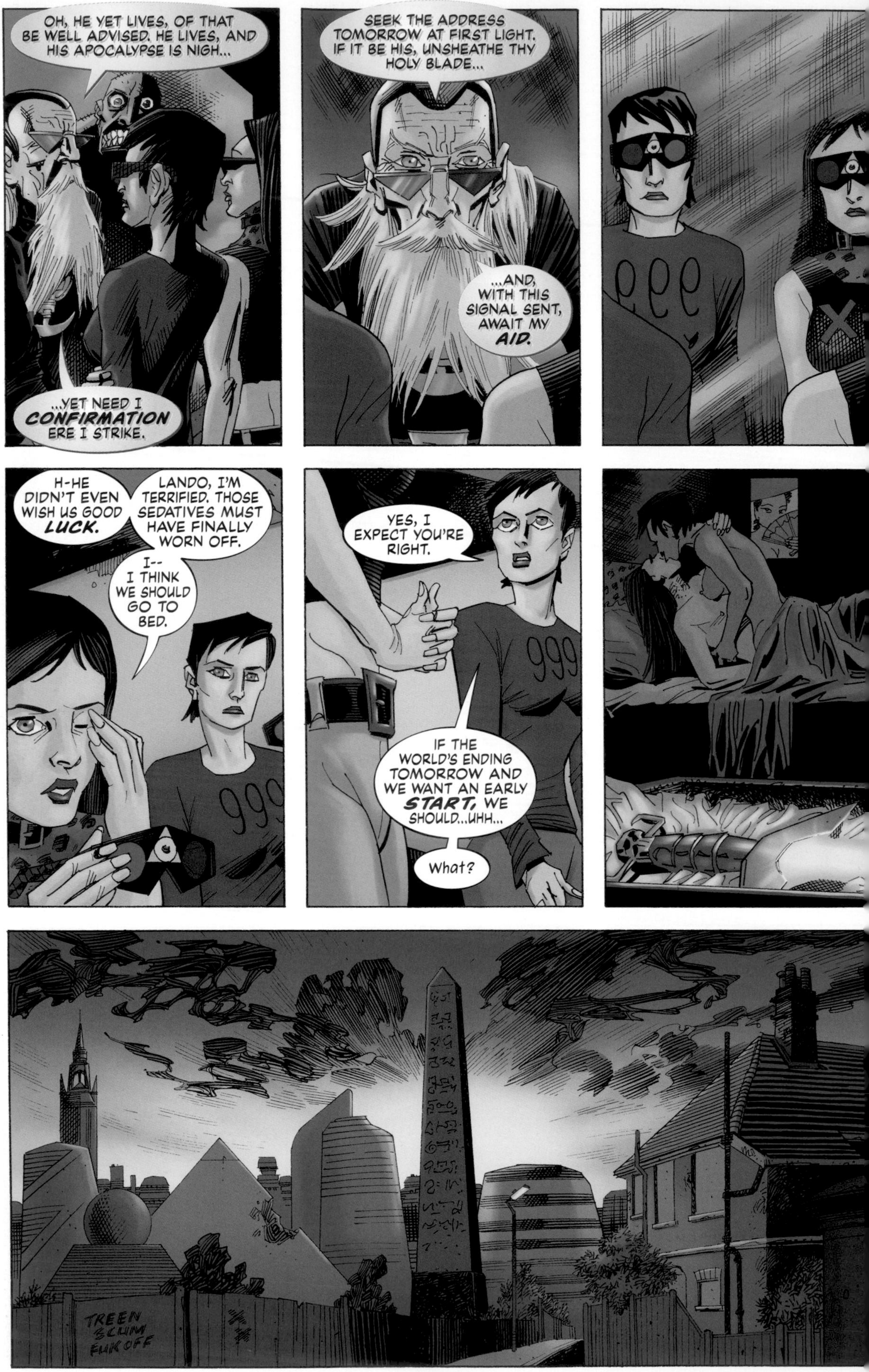
OH, HE YET LIVES, OF THAT BE WELL ADVISED. HE LIVES, AND HIS APOCALYPSE IS NIGH...
...YET NEED I CONFIRMATION ERE I STRIKE.
SEEK THE ADDRESS TOMORROW AT FIRST LIGHT. IF IT BE HIS, UNSHEATHE THY HOLY BLADE...
...AND, WITH THIS SIGNAL SENT, AWAIT MY AID.
H-HE DIDN'T EVEN WISH US GOOD LUCK.
LANDO, I'M TERRIFIED. THOSE SEDATIVES MUST HAVE FINALLY WORN OFF.
I-- I THINK WE SHOULD GO TO BED.
YES, I EXPECT YOU'RE RIGHT.
IF THE WORLD'S ENDING TOMORROW AND WE WANT AN EARLY START, WE SHOULD...UHH...
What?
TREEN SCUM FUK OFF

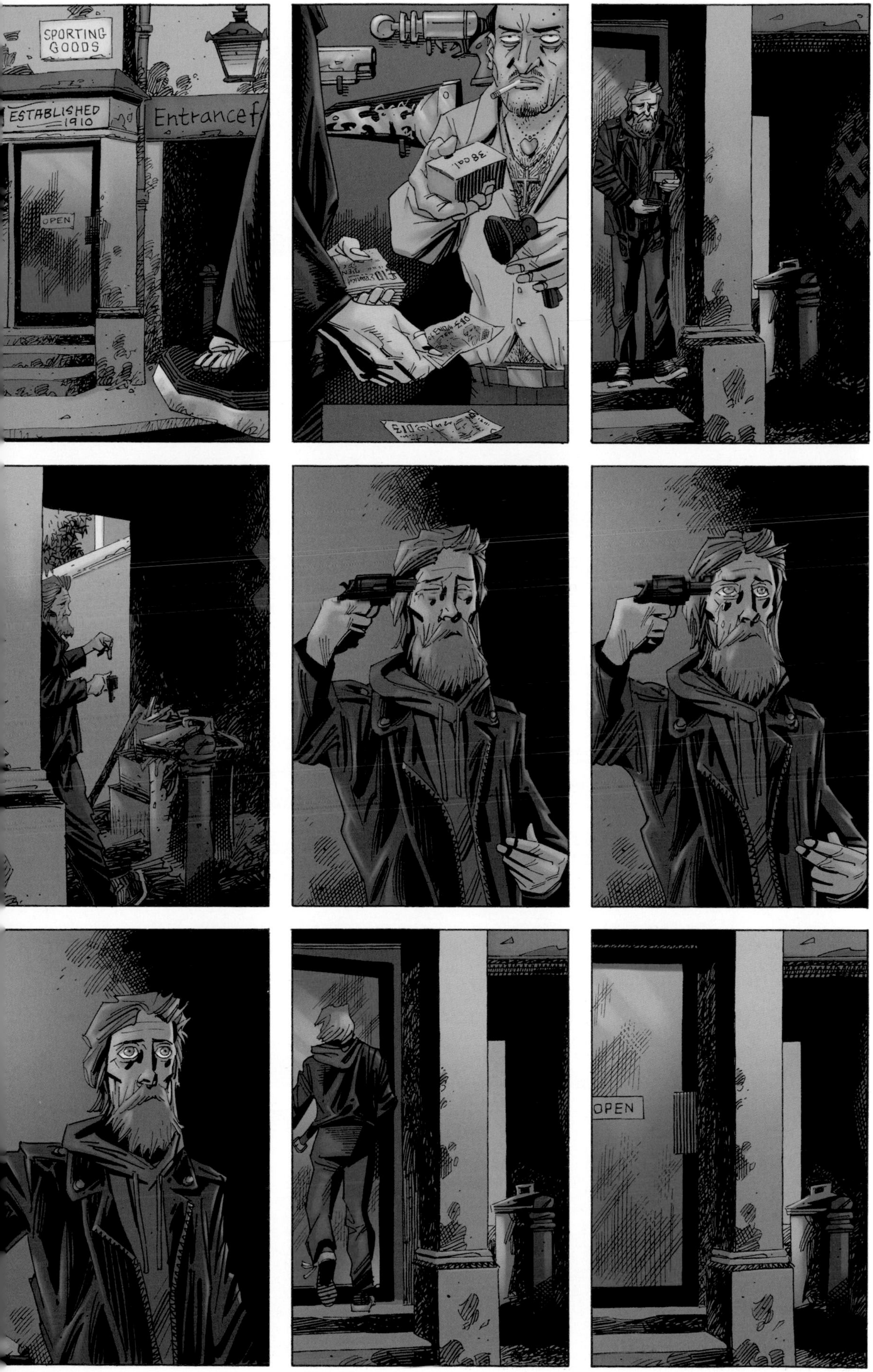
SPORTING GOODS
ESTABLISHED 1910
Entrance f
OPEN
38 cal.
OPEN

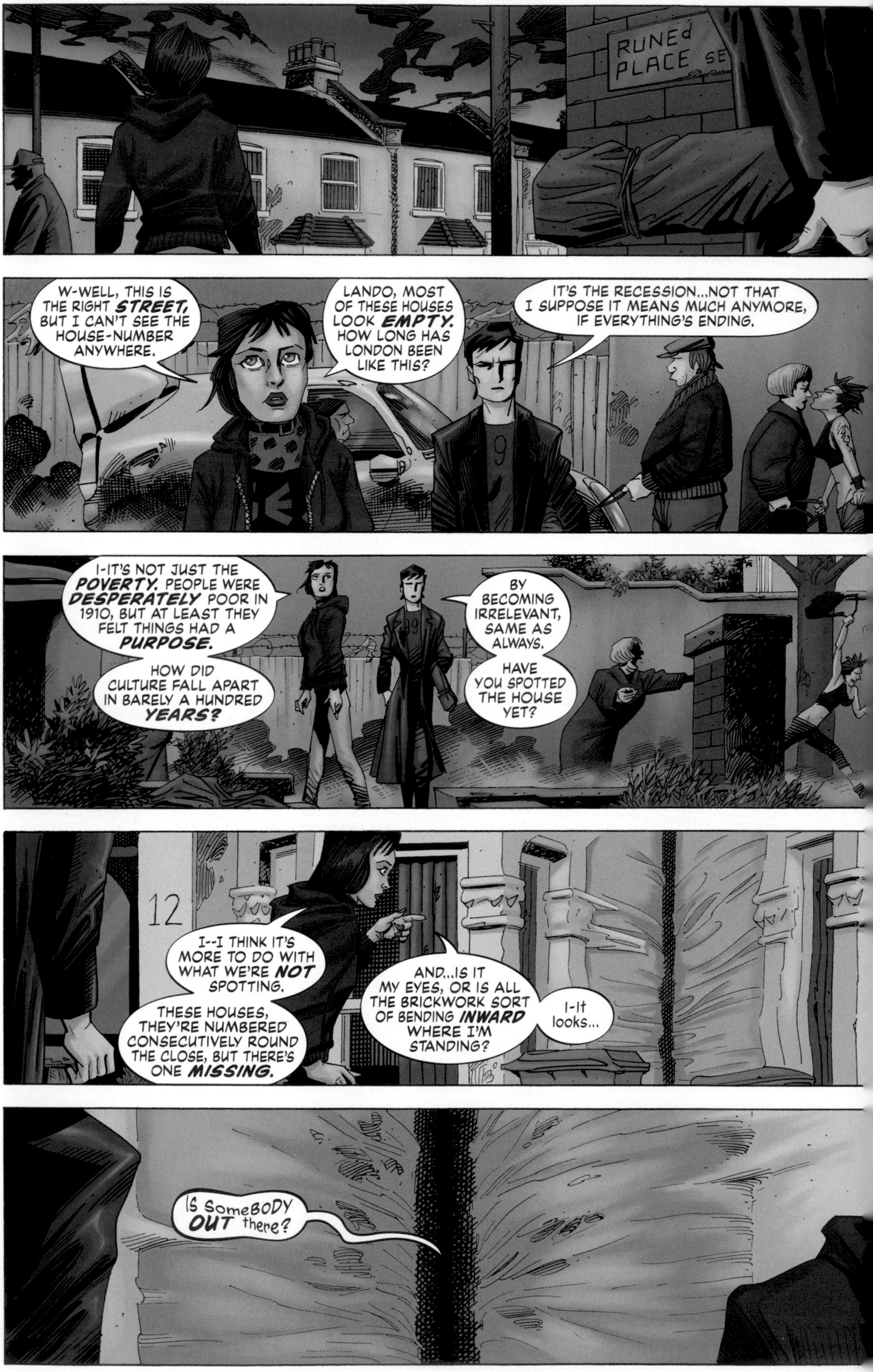
RUNEd PLACE SE
W-WELL, THIS IS THE RIGHT STREET, BUT I CAN'T SEE THE HOUSE-NUMBER ANYWHERE.
LANDO, MOST OF THESE HOUSES LOOK EMPTY. HOW LONG HAS LONDON BEEN LIKE THIS?
IT'S THE RECESSION...NOT THAT I SUPPOSE IT MEANS MUCH ANYMORE, IF EVERYTHING'S ENDING.
I-IT'S NOT JUST THE POVERTY. PEOPLE WERE DESPERATELY POOR IN 1910, BUT AT LEAST THEY FELT THINGS HAD A PURPOSE.
HOW DID CULTURE FALL APART IN BARELY A HUNDRED YEARS?
BY BECOMING IRRELEVANT, SAME AS ALWAYS.
HAVE YOU SPOTTED THE HOUSE YET?
12
I--I THINK IT'S MORE TO DO WITH WHAT WE'RE NOT SPOTTING.
THESE HOUSES, THEY'RE NUMBERED CONSECUTIVELY ROUND THE CLOSE, BUT THERE'S ONE MISSING.
AND...IS IT MY EYES, OR IS ALL THE BRICKWORK SORT OF BENDING INWARD WHERE I'M STANDING?
I-It looks...
Is SomeBODY OUT there?

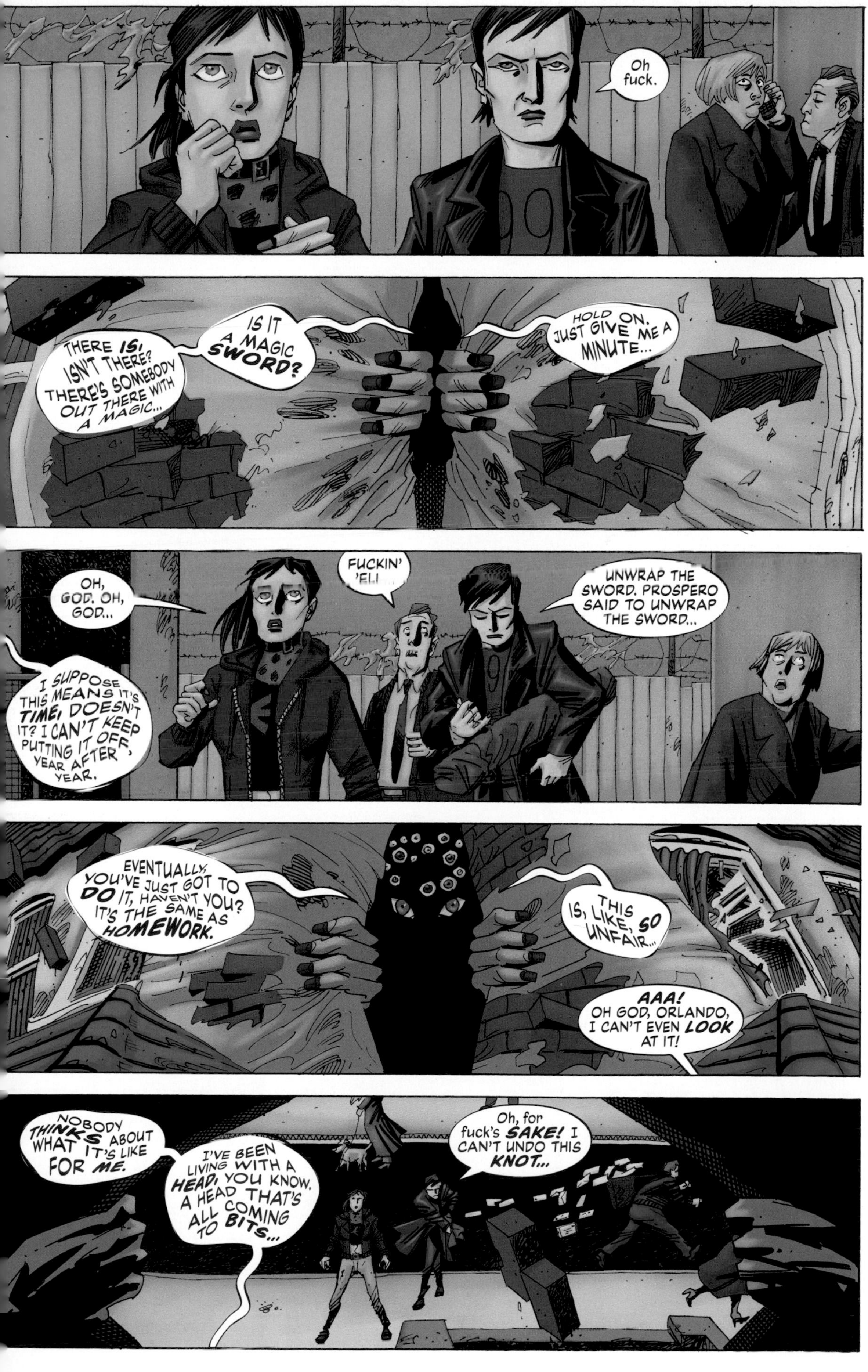
Oh fuck.
THERE IS, ISN'T THERE? THERE'S SOMEBODY OUT THERE WITH A MAGIC...
IS IT A MAGIC SWORD?
HOLD ON. JUST GIVE ME A MINUTE...
OH, GOD. OH, GOD...
FUCKIN' 'ELL
UNWRAP THE SWORD. PROSPERO SAID TO UNWRAP THE SWORD...
I SUPPOSE THIS MEANS IT'S TIME, DOESN'T IT? I CAN'T KEEP PUTTING IT OFF, YEAR AFTER YEAR.
EVENTUALLY, YOU'VE JUST GOT TO DO IT, HAVEN'T YOU? IT'S THE SAME AS HOMEWORK.
THIS IS, LIKE, SO UNFAIR...
AAA! OH GOD, ORLANDO, I CAN'T EVEN LOOK AT IT!
NOBODY THINKS ABOUT WHAT IT'S LIKE FOR ME.
I'VE BEEN LIVING WITH A HEAD, YOU KNOW. A HEAD THAT'S ALL COMING TO BITS...
Oh, for fuck's SAKE! I CAN'T UNDO THIS KNOT...

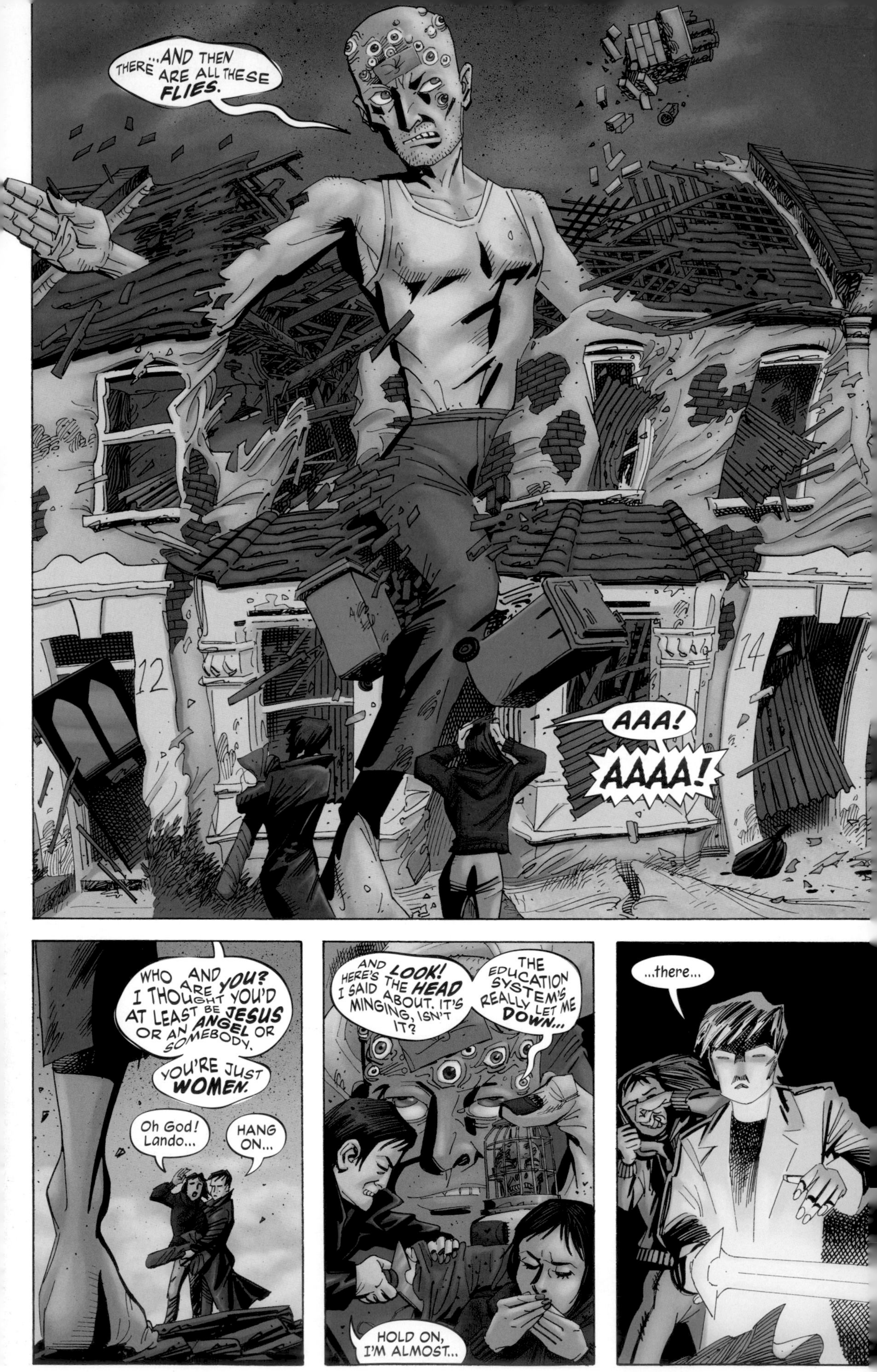
...AND THEN THERE ARE ALL THESE FLIES.
AAA!
AAAA!
WHO ARE YOU? AND I THOUGHT YOU'D AT LEAST BE JESUS OR AN ANGEL OR SOMEBODY.
YOU'RE JUST WOMEN.
Oh God! Lando...
HANG ON...
LOOK! AND HERE'S THE HEAD I SAID ABOUT. IT'S MINGING, ISN'T IT?
THE EDUCATION SYSTEM'S REALLY LET ME DOWN...
HOLD ON, I'M ALMOST...
...there...

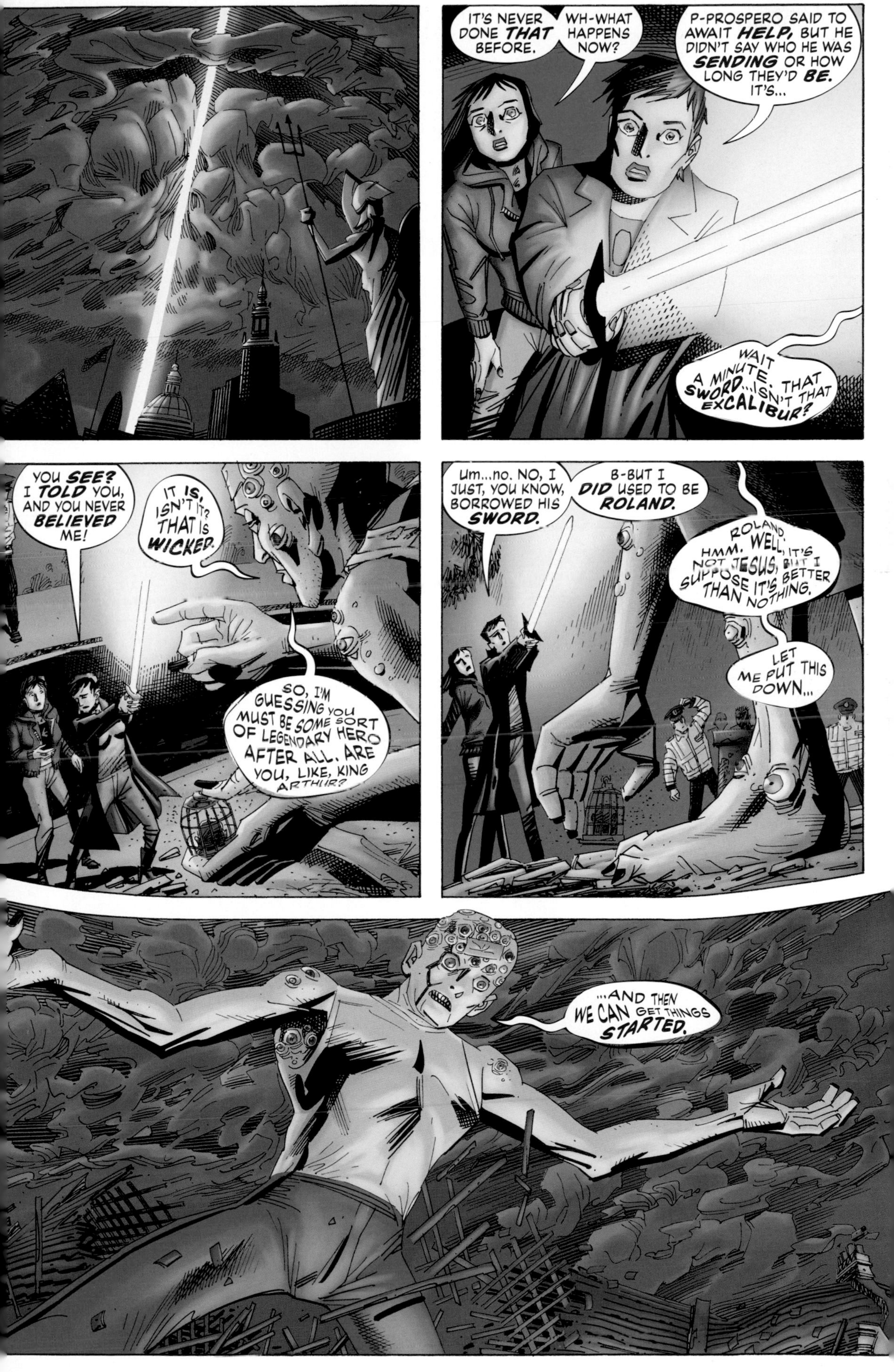
IT'S NEVER DONE THAT BEFORE.
WH-WHAT HAPPENS NOW?
P-PROSPERO SAID TO AWAIT HELP, BUT HE DIDN'T SAY WHO HE WAS SENDING OR HOW LONG THEY'D BE. IT'S...
WAIT A MINUTE. THAT SWORD...ISN'T THAT EXCALIBUR?
YOU SEE? I TOLD YOU, AND YOU NEVER BELIEVED ME!
IT IS, ISN'T IT? THAT IS WICKED.
SO, I'M GUESSING YOU MUST BE SOME SORT OF LEGENDARY HERO AFTER ALL. ARE YOU, LIKE, KING ARTHUR?
Um...no. NO, I JUST, YOU KNOW, BORROWED HIS SWORD.
B-BUT I DID USED TO BE ROLAND.
ROLAND. HMM. WELL, IT'S NOT JESUS, BUT I SUPPOSE IT'S BETTER THAN NOTHING.
LET ME PUT THIS DOWN...
...AND THEN WE CAN GET THINGS STARTED.

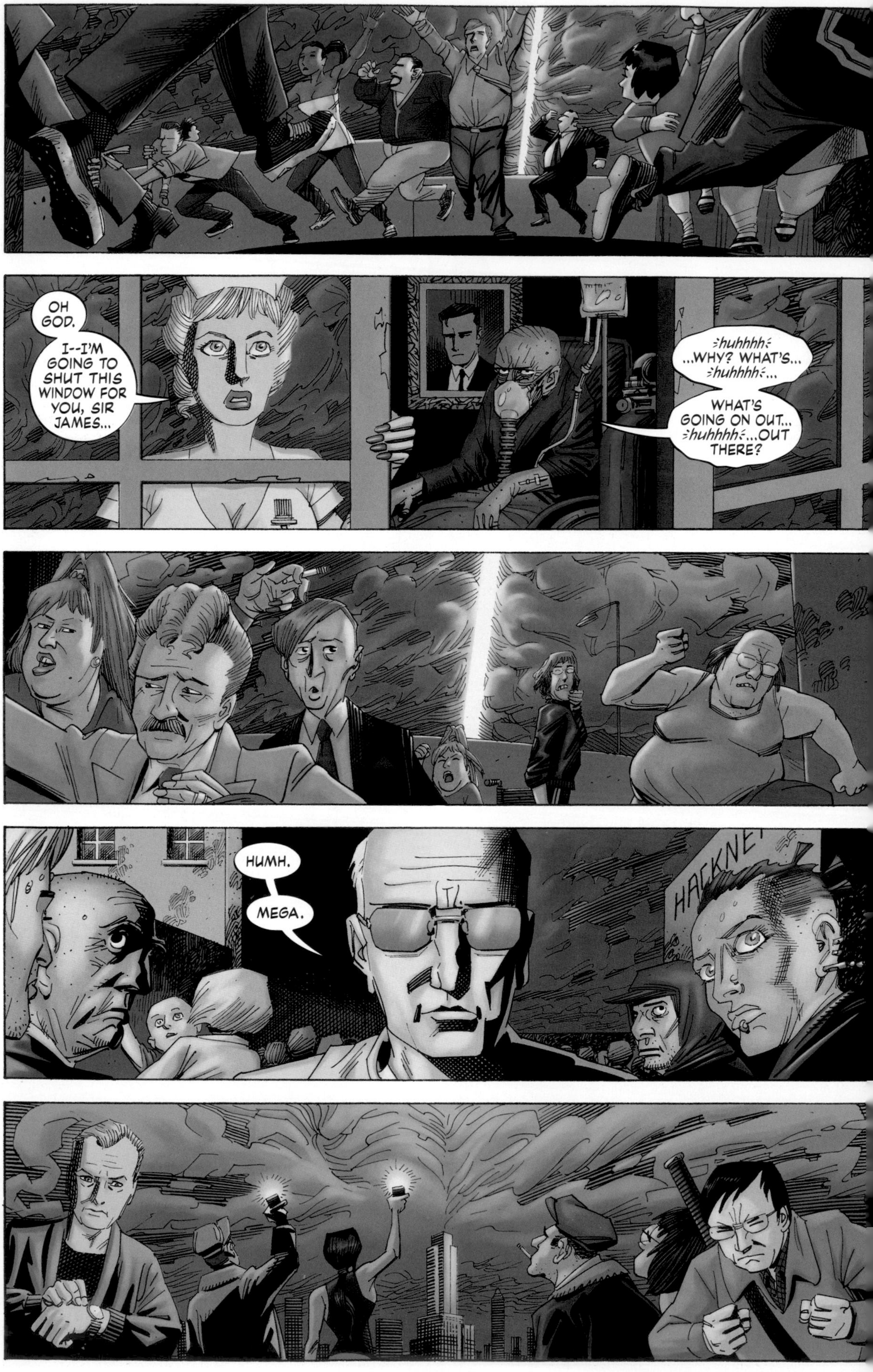
OH GOD.
I--I'M GOING TO SHUT THIS WINDOW FOR YOU, SIR JAMES...
huhhhh ...WHY? WHAT'S... huhhhh...
WHAT'S GOING ON OUT... huhhhh ...OUT THERE?
HUMH.
MEGA.

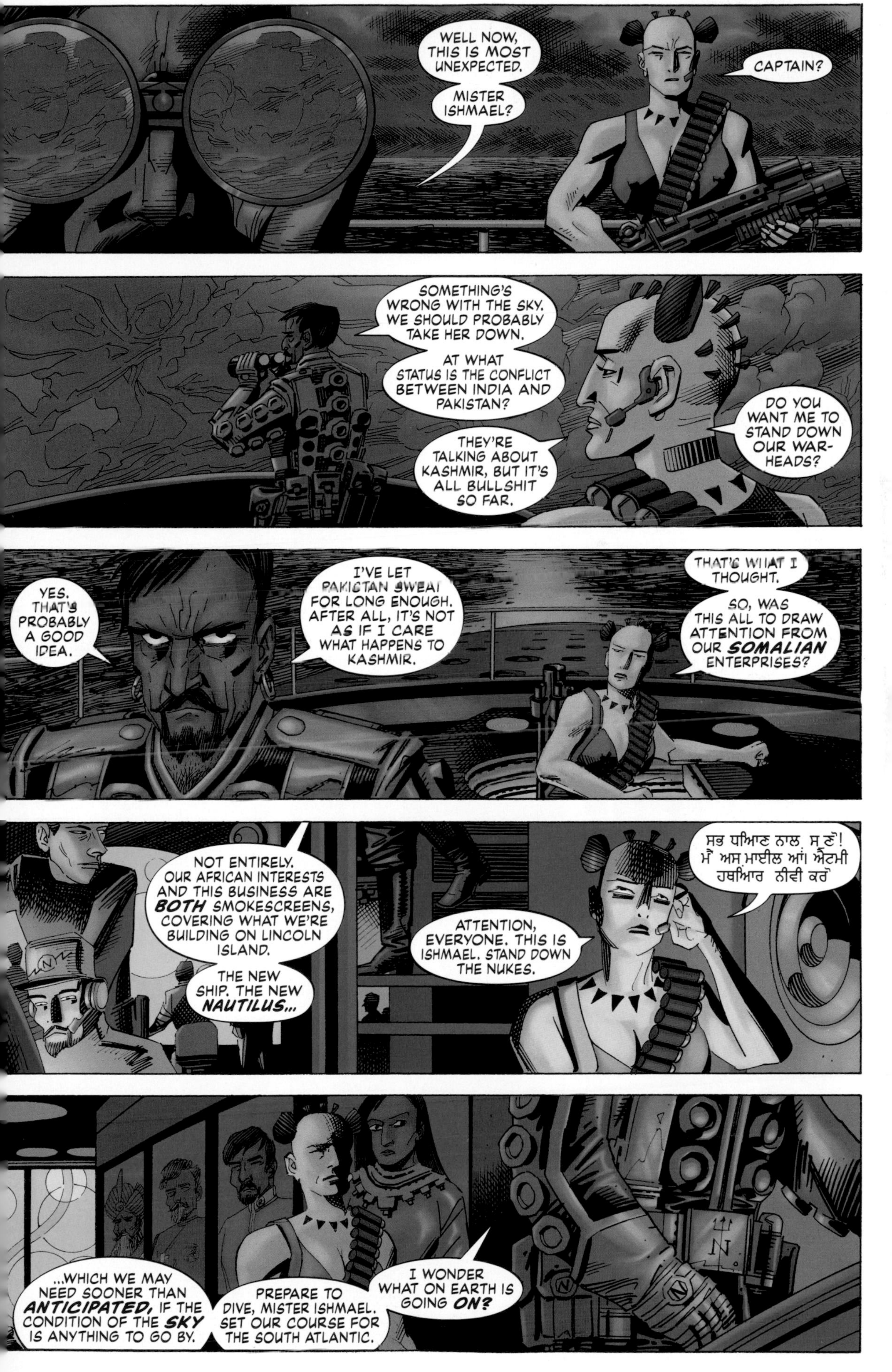
WELL NOW, THIS IS MOST UNEXPECTED.
MISTER ISHMAEL?
CAPTAIN?
SOMETHING'S WRONG WITH THE SKY. WE SHOULD PROBABLY TAKE HER DOWN.
AT WHAT STATUS IS THE CONFLICT BETWEEN INDIA AND PAKISTAN?
THEY'RE TALKING ABOUT KASHMIR, BUT IT'S ALL BULLSHIT SO FAR.
DO YOU WANT ME TO STAND DOWN OUR WAR-HEADS?
YES. THAT'S PROBABLY A GOOD IDEA.
I'VE LET PAKISTAN SWEAT FOR LONG ENOUGH. AFTER ALL, IT'S NOT AS IF I CARE WHAT HAPPENS TO KASHMIR.
THAT'S WHAT I THOUGHT.
SO, WAS THIS ALL TO DRAW ATTENTION FROM OUR **SOMALIAN** ENTERPRISES?
NOT ENTIRELY. OUR AFRICAN INTERESTS AND THIS BUSINESS ARE **BOTH** SMOKESCREENS, COVERING WHAT WE'RE BUILDING ON LINCOLN ISLAND.
THE NEW SHIP. THE NEW **NAUTILUS...**
ਸਭ ਧਿਆਣ ਨਾਲ ਸੁਣੋ! ਮੈਂ ਅਸ਼ਮਾਈਲ ਆਂ। ਐਟਮੀ ਹਥਿਆਰ ਨੀਵੀ ਕਰੋ
ATTENTION, EVERYONE. THIS IS ISHMAEL. STAND DOWN THE NUKES.
...WHICH WE MAY NEED SOONER THAN **ANTICIPATED,** IF THE CONDITION OF THE **SKY** IS ANYTHING TO GO BY.
PREPARE TO DIVE, MISTER ISHMAEL. SET OUR COURSE FOR THE SOUTH ATLANTIC.
I WONDER WHAT ON EARTH IS GOING **ON?**

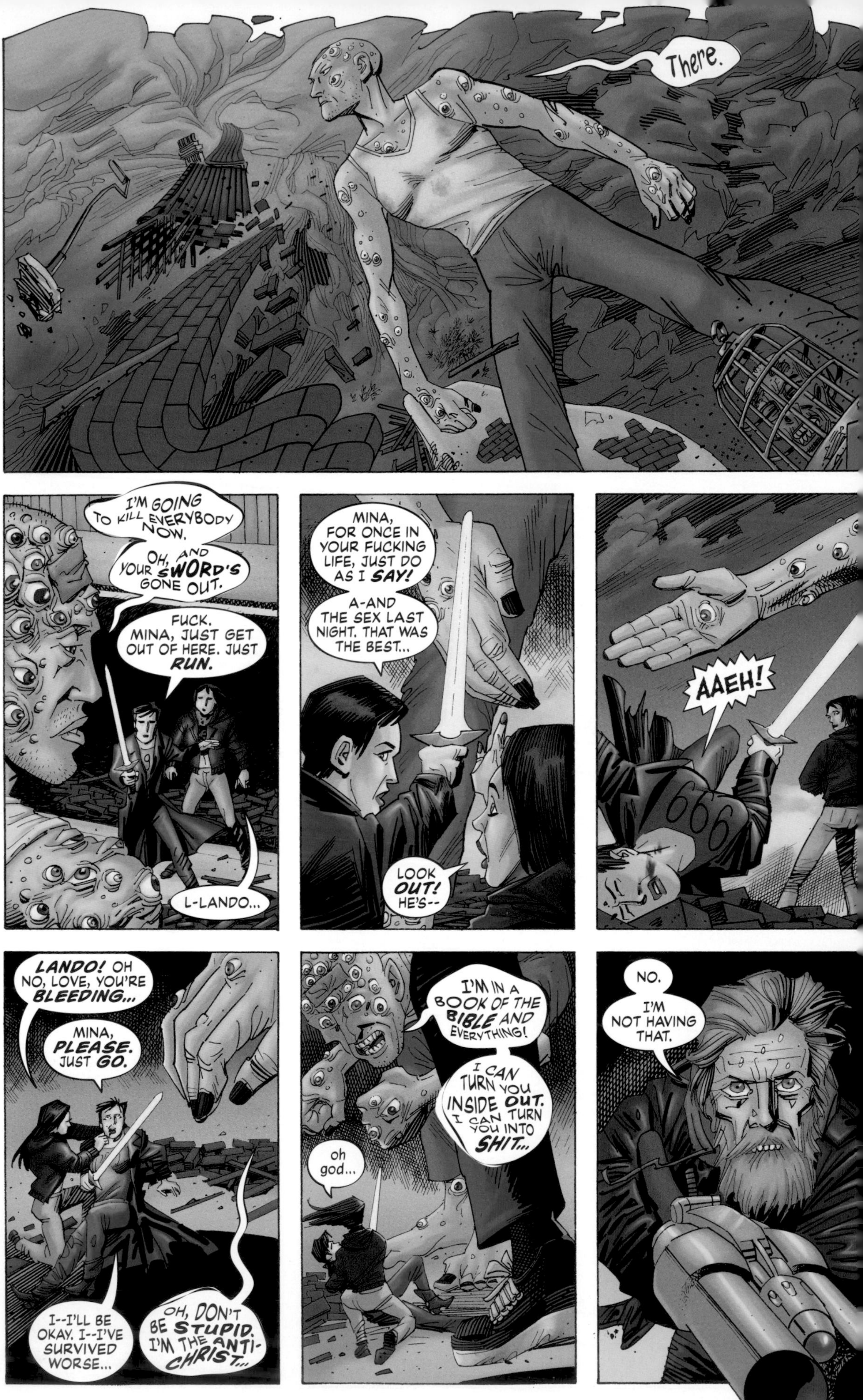
There.
I'M GOING TO KILL EVERYBODY NOW.
OH, AND YOUR SWORD'S GONE OUT.
FUCK. MINA, JUST GET OUT OF HERE. JUST RUN.
L-LANDO...
MINA, FOR ONCE IN YOUR FUCKING LIFE, JUST DO AS I SAY!
A-AND THE SEX LAST NIGHT. THAT WAS THE BEST...
LOOK OUT! HE'S--
AAEH!
LANDO! OH NO, LOVE, YOU'RE BLEEDING...
MINA, PLEASE. JUST GO.
I--I'LL BE OKAY. I--I'VE SURVIVED WORSE...
OH, DON'T BE STUPID. I'M THE ANTI-CHRIST...
I'M IN A BOOK OF THE BIBLE AND EVERYTHING!
I CAN TURN YOU INSIDE OUT. I CAN TURN YOU INTO SHIT...
oh god...
NO.
I'M NOT HAVING THAT.

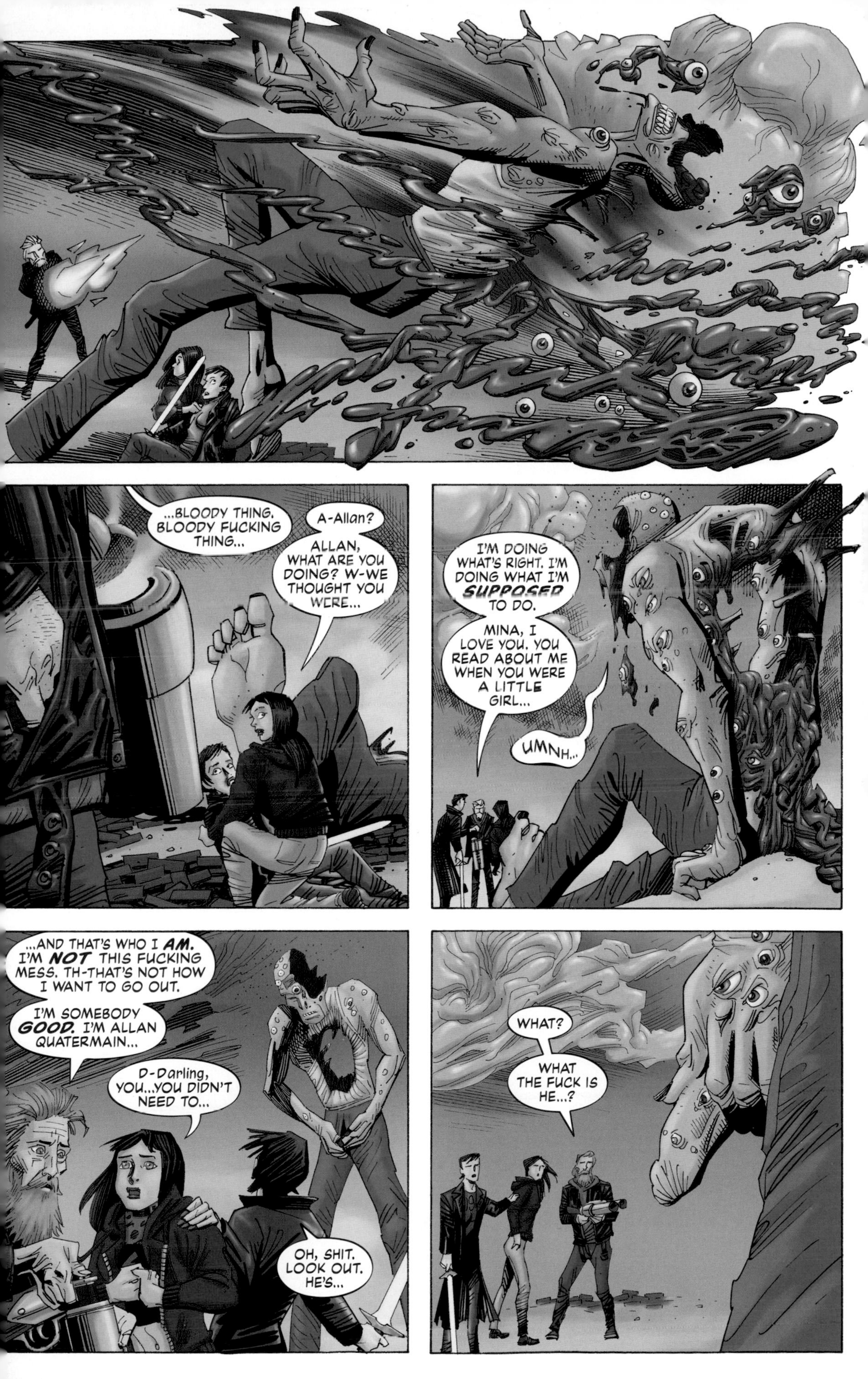
...BLOODY THING. BLOODY FUCKING THING...
A-Allan?
ALLAN, WHAT ARE YOU DOING? W-WE THOUGHT YOU WERE...
I'M DOING WHAT'S RIGHT. I'M DOING WHAT I'M SUPPOSED TO DO.
MINA, I LOVE YOU. YOU READ ABOUT ME WHEN YOU WERE A LITTLE GIRL...
UMNH...
...AND THAT'S WHO I AM. I'M NOT THIS FUCKING MESS. TH-THAT'S NOT HOW I WANT TO GO OUT.
I'M SOMEBODY GOOD. I'M ALLAN QUATERMAIN...
D-Darling, YOU...YOU DIDN'T NEED TO...
OH, SHIT. LOOK OUT. HE'S...
WHAT?
WHAT THE FUCK IS HE...?

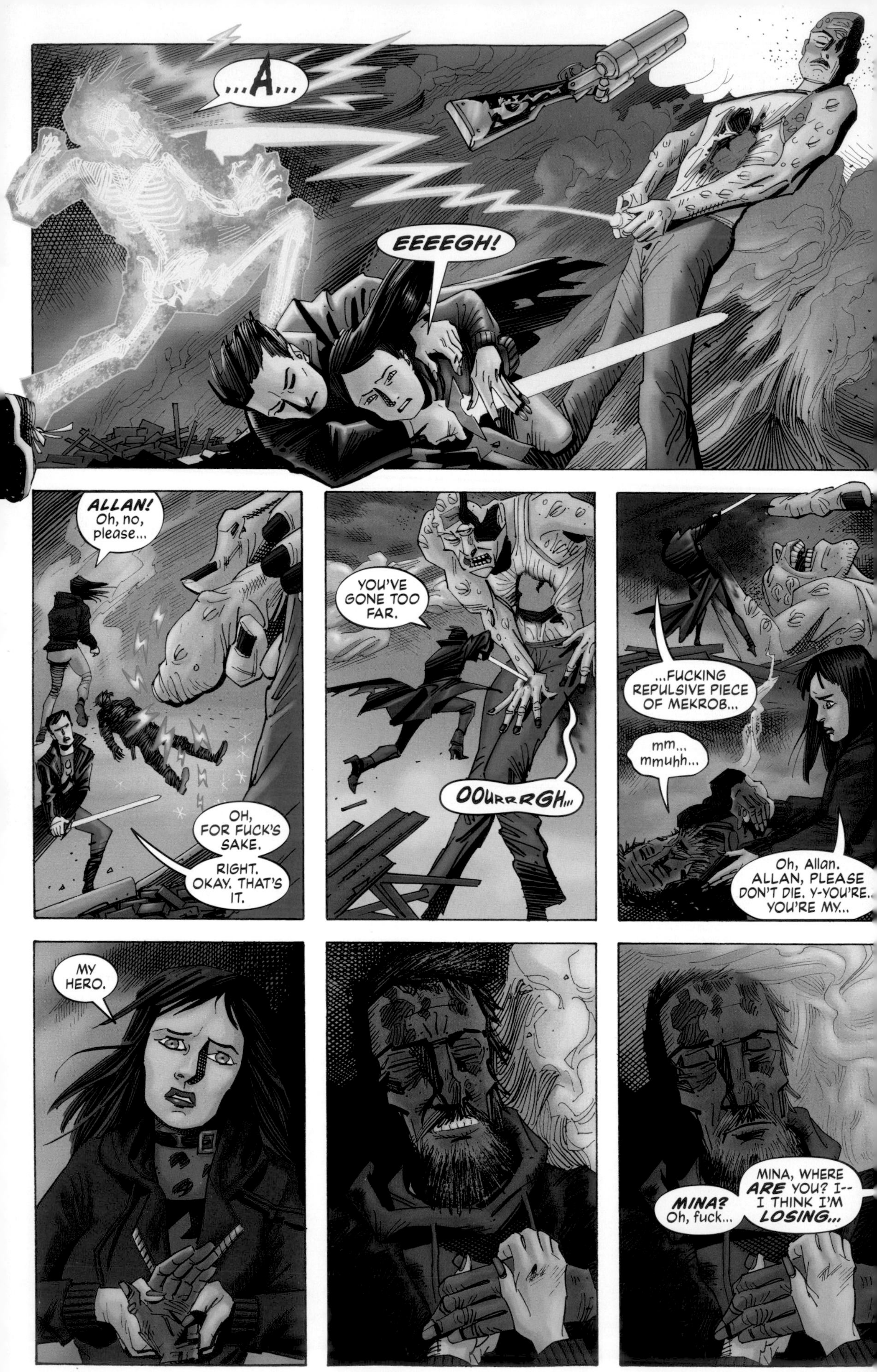
...A...
EEEEGH!
ALLAN! Oh, no, please...
OH, FOR FUCK'S SAKE.
RIGHT. OKAY. THAT'S IT.
YOU'VE GONE TOO FAR.
OOURRRGH...
...FUCKING REPULSIVE PIECE OF MEKROB...
mm... mmuhh...
Oh, Allan. ALLAN, PLEASE DON'T DIE. Y-YOU'RE... YOU'RE MY...
MY HERO.
MINA? Oh, fuck...
MINA, WHERE ARE YOU? I-- I THINK I'M LOSING...

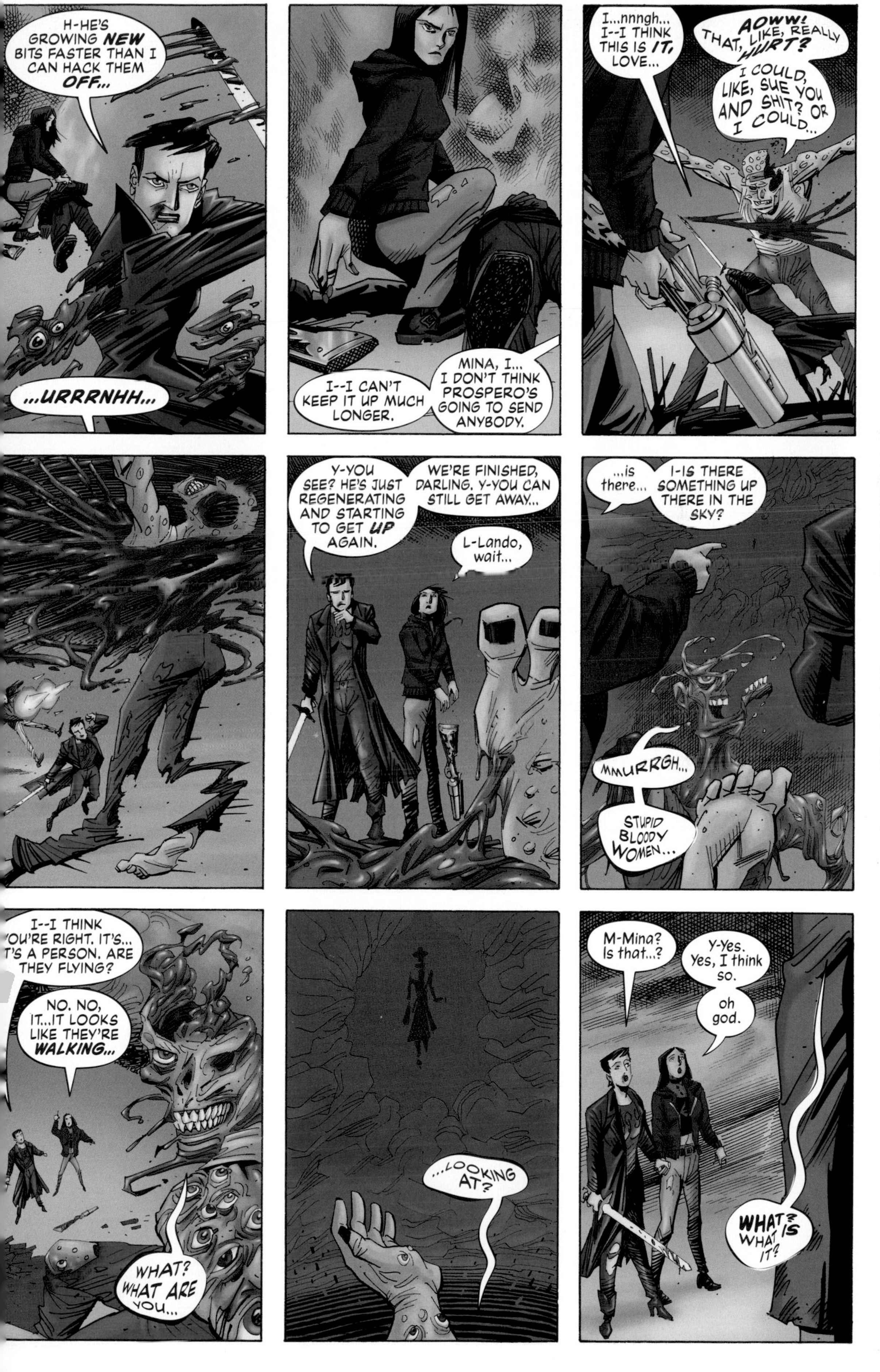
H-HE'S GROWING NEW BITS FASTER THAN I CAN HACK THEM OFF...
...URRRNHH...
I--I CAN'T KEEP IT UP MUCH LONGER.
MINA, I... I DON'T THINK PROSPERO'S GOING TO SEND ANYBODY.
I...nnngh... I--I THINK THIS IS IT, LOVE...
AOWW! THAT, LIKE, REALLY HURT?
I COULD, LIKE, SUE YOU AND SHIT? OR I COULD...
Y-YOU SEE? HE'S JUST REGENERATING AND STARTING TO GET UP AGAIN.
WE'RE FINISHED, DARLING. Y-YOU CAN STILL GET AWAY...
L-Lando, wait...
...is there...
I-IS THERE SOMETHING UP THERE IN THE SKY?
MMURRGH...
STUPID BLOODY WOMEN...
I--I THINK YOU'RE RIGHT. IT'S... IT'S A PERSON. ARE THEY FLYING?
NO. NO, IT...IT LOOKS LIKE THEY'RE WALKING...
WHAT? WHAT ARE YOU...
...LOOKING AT?
M-Mina? Is that...?
Y-Yes. Yes, I think so.
oh god.
WHAT? WHAT IS IT?

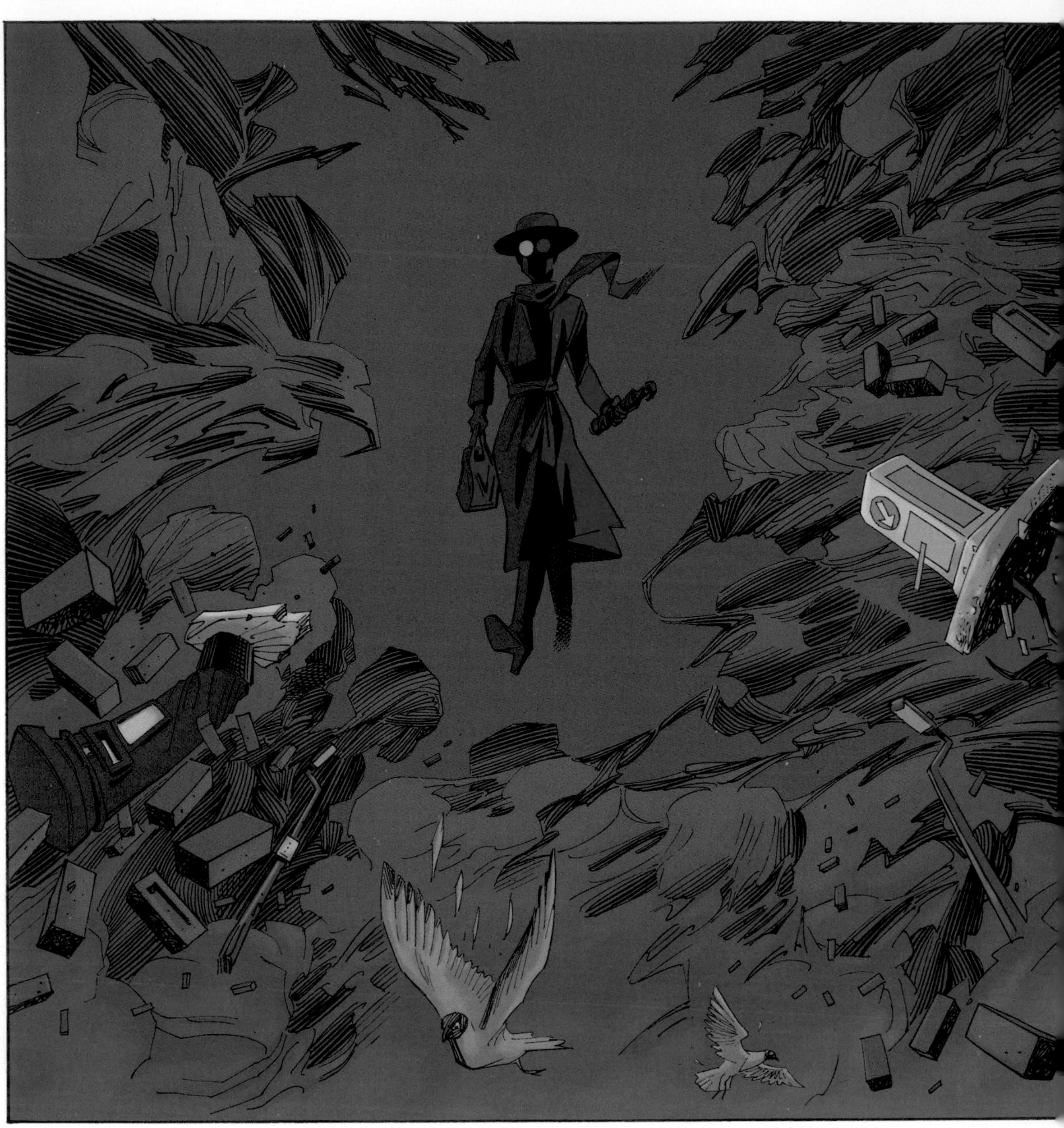

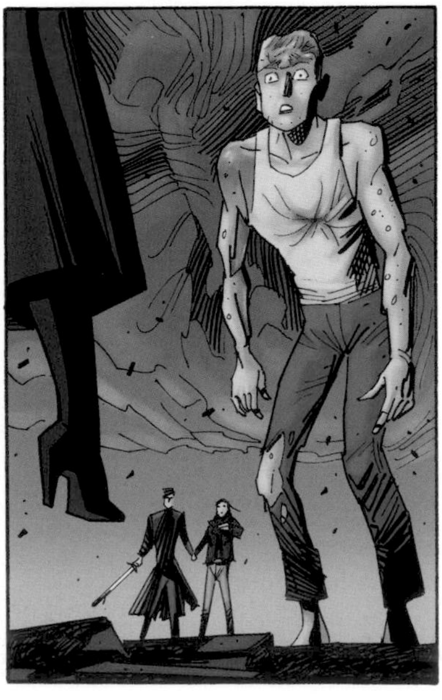

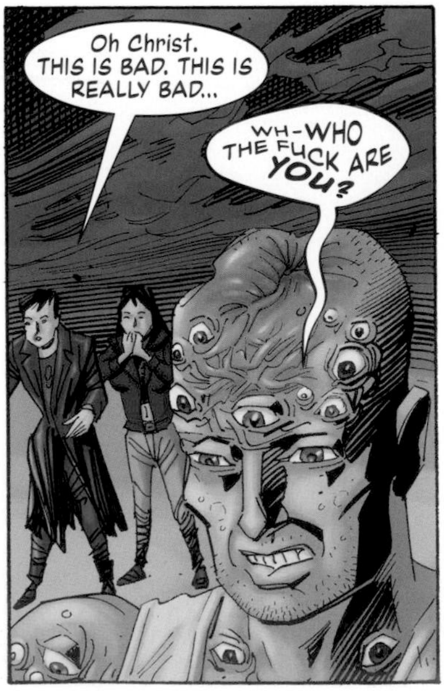
Oh Christ.
THIS IS BAD. THIS IS
REALLY BAD...
WH-WHO
THE FUCK ARE
YOU?

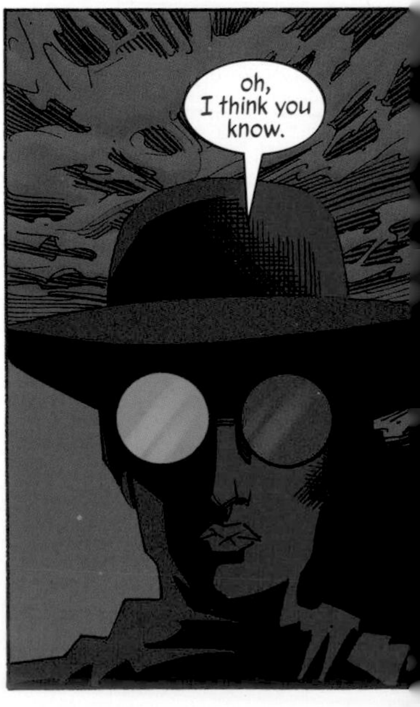
oh,
I think you
know.

I have a great many responsibilities.

foremost amongst these, however, is my concern for children.

I am concerned regarding their wellbeing, and the healthy development of their imaginations.

I am concerned regarding their behaviour...

...and I'm afraid, young man, that I don't care for you at all.

THAT IS, LIKE, TOTALLY DISRESPECTING ME, YEAH? I MEAN, YOU KNOW THAT I'M, LIKE, THE ANTICHRIST AND EVERYTHING?

I'M WELL FAMOUS, ACTUALLY, I'M IN A BOOK OF THE BIBLE!

tsk. just the one book?

I'm on every page.

who did you think you were talking to?

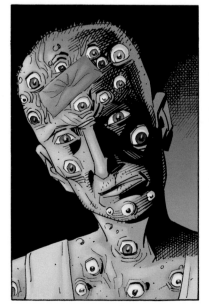

GLUP.

HCCCH...

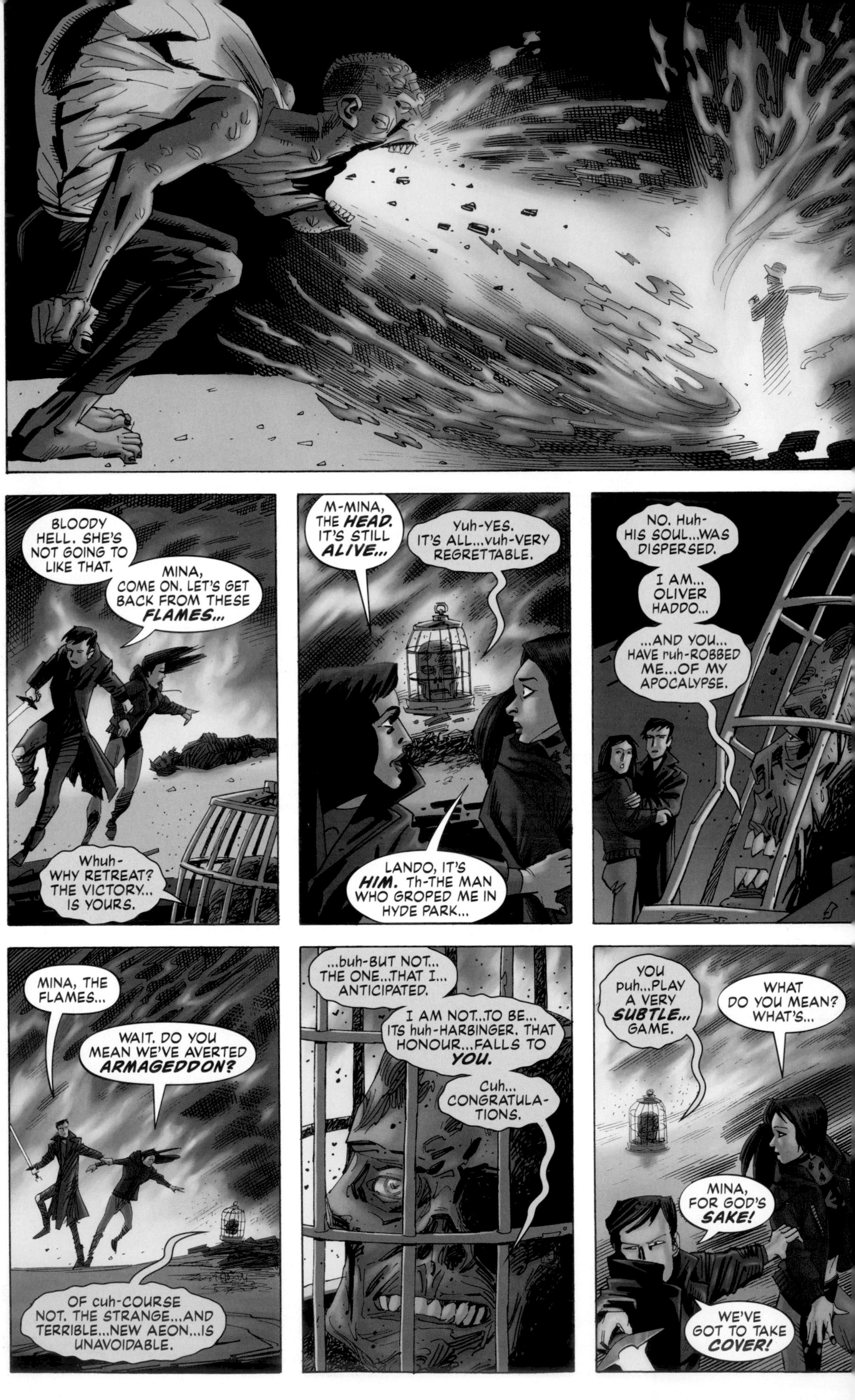
BLOODY HELL. SHE'S NOT GOING TO LIKE THAT.
MINA, COME ON. LET'S GET BACK FROM THESE FLAMES...
Whuh-WHY RETREAT? THE VICTORY... IS YOURS.
M-MINA, THE HEAD. IT'S STILL ALIVE...
Yuh-YES. IT'S ALL...vuh-VERY REGRETTABLE.
LANDO, IT'S HIM. Th-THE MAN WHO GROPED ME IN HYDE PARK...
NO. Huh-HIS SOUL...WAS DISPERSED.
I AM... OLIVER HADDO...
...AND YOU... HAVE ruh-ROBBED ME...OF MY APOCALYPSE.
MINA, THE FLAMES...
WAIT. DO YOU MEAN WE'VE AVERTED ARMAGEDDON?
OF cuh-COURSE NOT. THE STRANGE...AND TERRIBLE...NEW AEON...IS UNAVOIDABLE.
...buh-BUT NOT... THE ONE...THAT I... ANTICIPATED.
I AM NOT...TO BE... ITS huh-HARBINGER. THAT HONOUR...FALLS TO YOU.
Cuh... CONGRATULA-TIONS.
YOU puh...PLAY A VERY SUBTLE... GAME.
WHAT DO YOU MEAN? WHAT'S...
MINA, FOR GOD'S SAKE!
WE'VE GOT TO TAKE COVER!

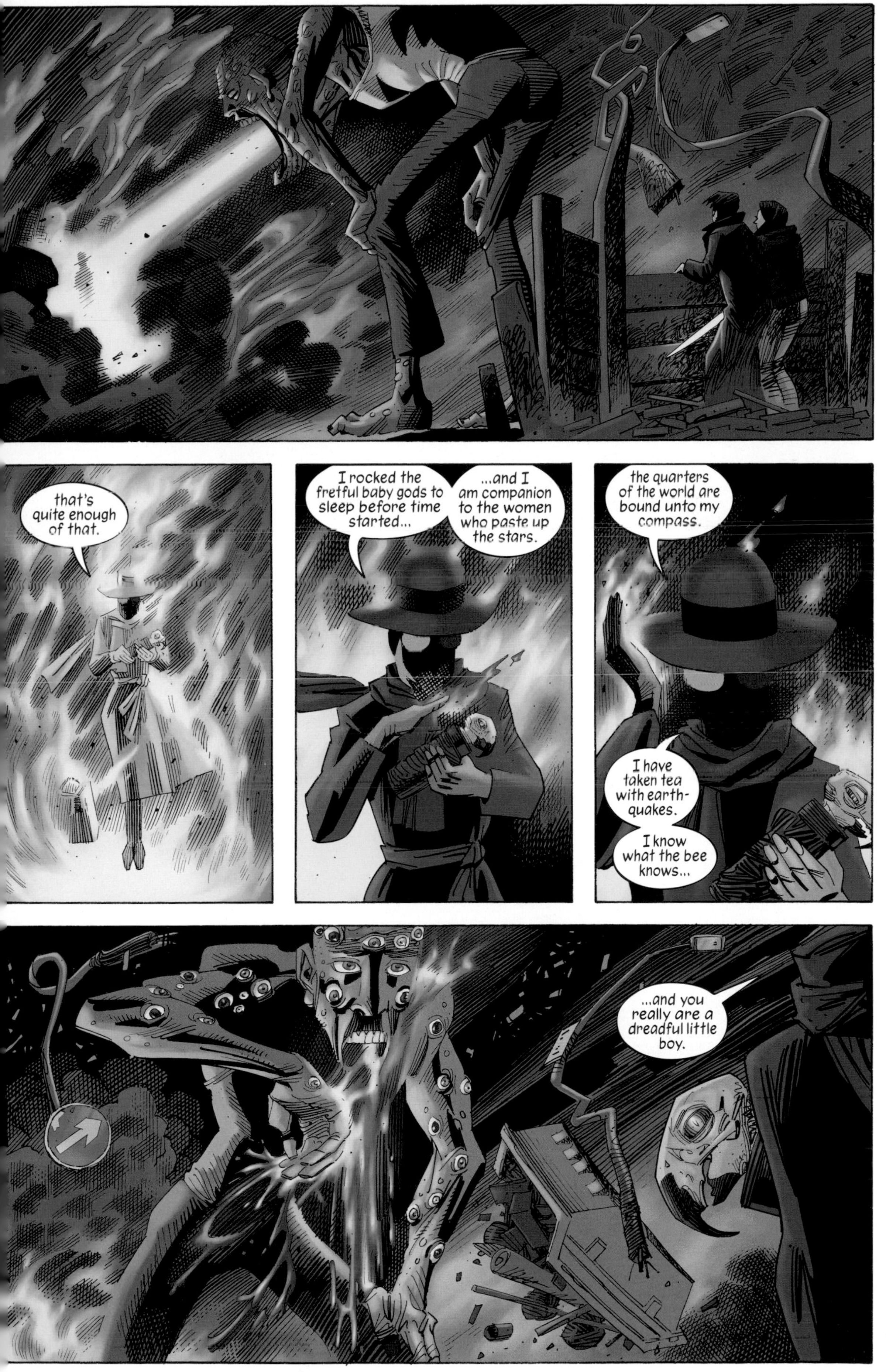
that's quite enough of that.
I rocked the fretful baby gods to sleep before time started...
...and I am companion to the women who paste up the stars.
the quarters of the world are bound unto my compass.
I have taken tea with earth-quakes.
I know what the bee knows...
...and you really are a dreadful little boy.

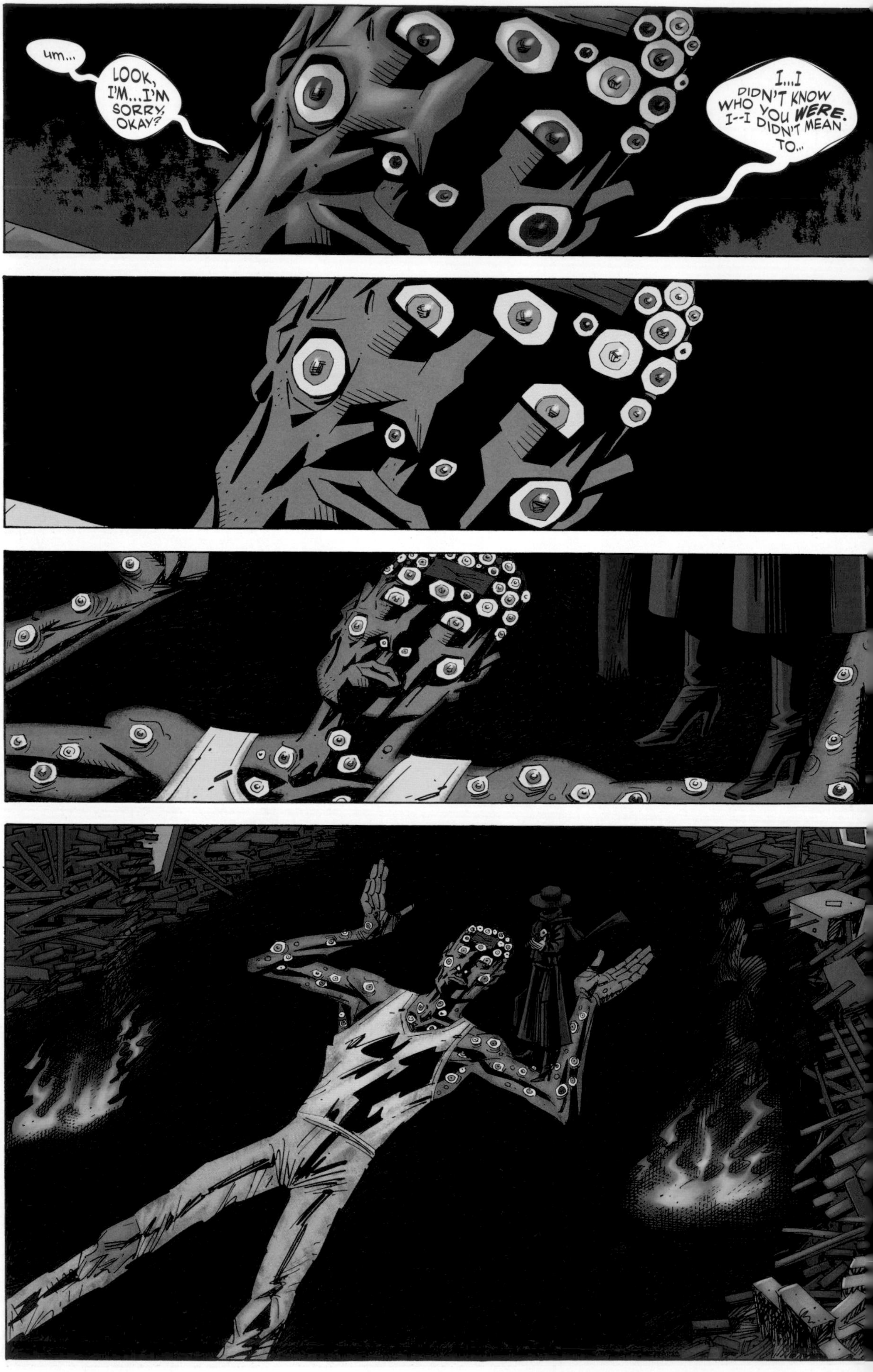
um...
LOOK, I'M...I'M SORRY, OKAY?
I...I DIDN'T KNOW WHO YOU WERE. I--I DIDN'T MEAN TO...

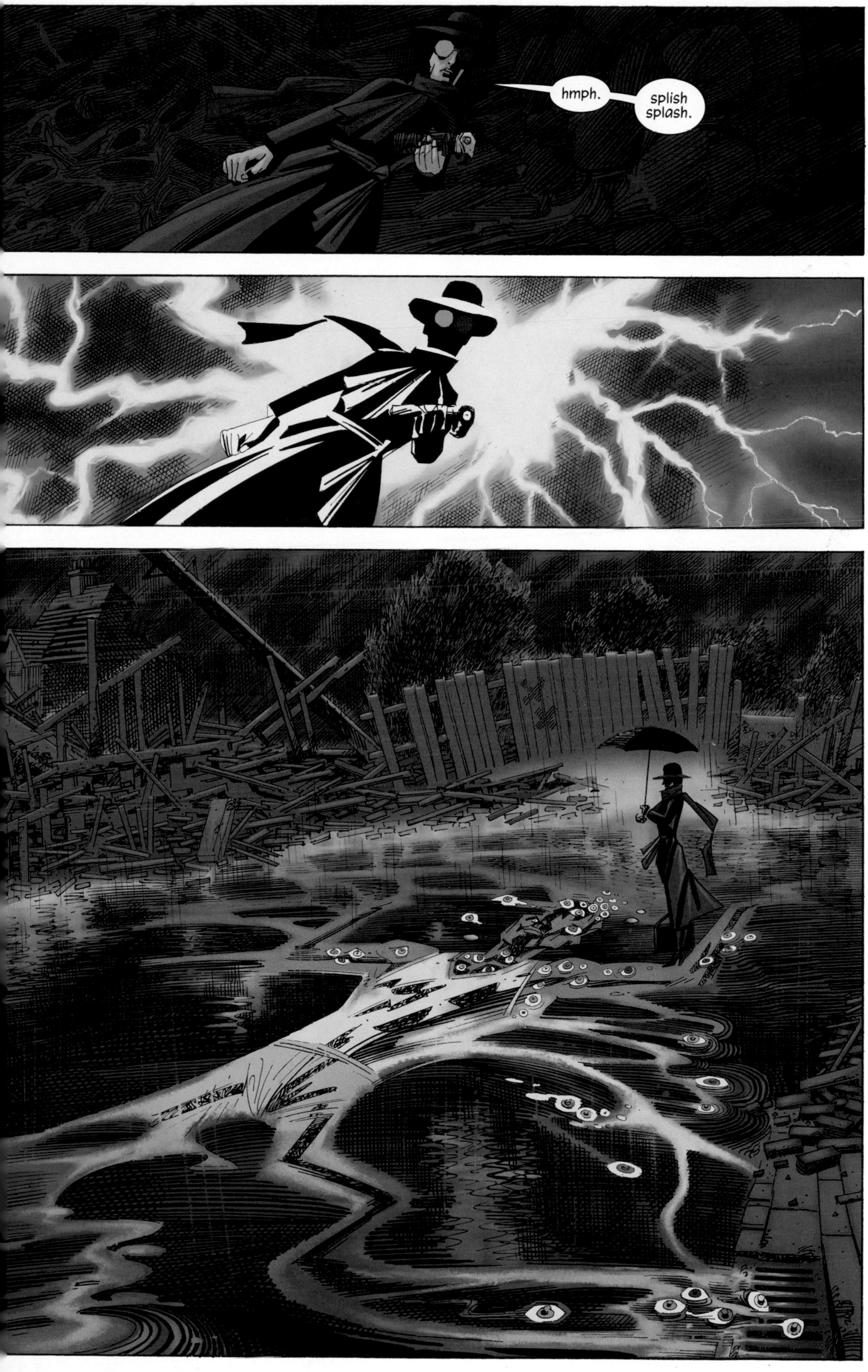
hmph.
splish
splash.

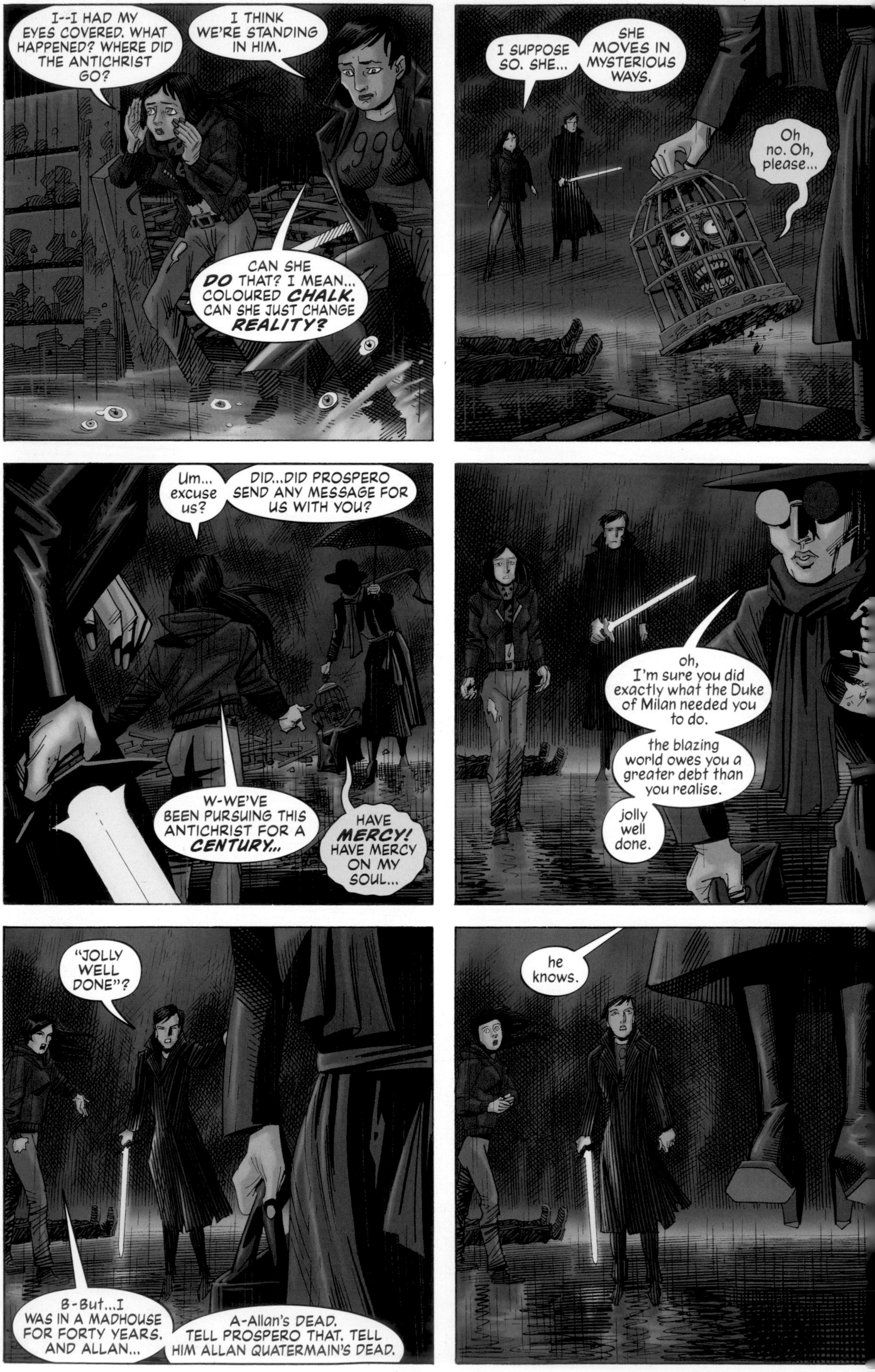
I--I HAD MY EYES COVERED. WHAT HAPPENED? WHERE DID THE ANTICHRIST GO?
I THINK WE'RE STANDING IN HIM.
CAN SHE DO THAT? I MEAN... COLOURED CHALK. CAN SHE JUST CHANGE REALITY?
I SUPPOSE SO. SHE...
SHE MOVES IN MYSTERIOUS WAYS.
Oh no. Oh, please...
Um... excuse us?
DID...DID PROSPERO SEND ANY MESSAGE FOR US WITH YOU?
W-WE'VE BEEN PURSUING THIS ANTICHRIST FOR A CENTURY...
HAVE MERCY! HAVE MERCY ON MY SOUL...
oh, I'm sure you did exactly what the Duke of Milan needed you to do.
the blazing world owes you a greater debt than you realise.
jolly well done.
"JOLLY WELL DONE"?
B-But...I WAS IN A MADHOUSE FOR FORTY YEARS. AND ALLAN...
A-Allan's DEAD. TELL PROSPERO THAT. TELL HIM ALLAN QUATERMAIN'S DEAD.
he knows.

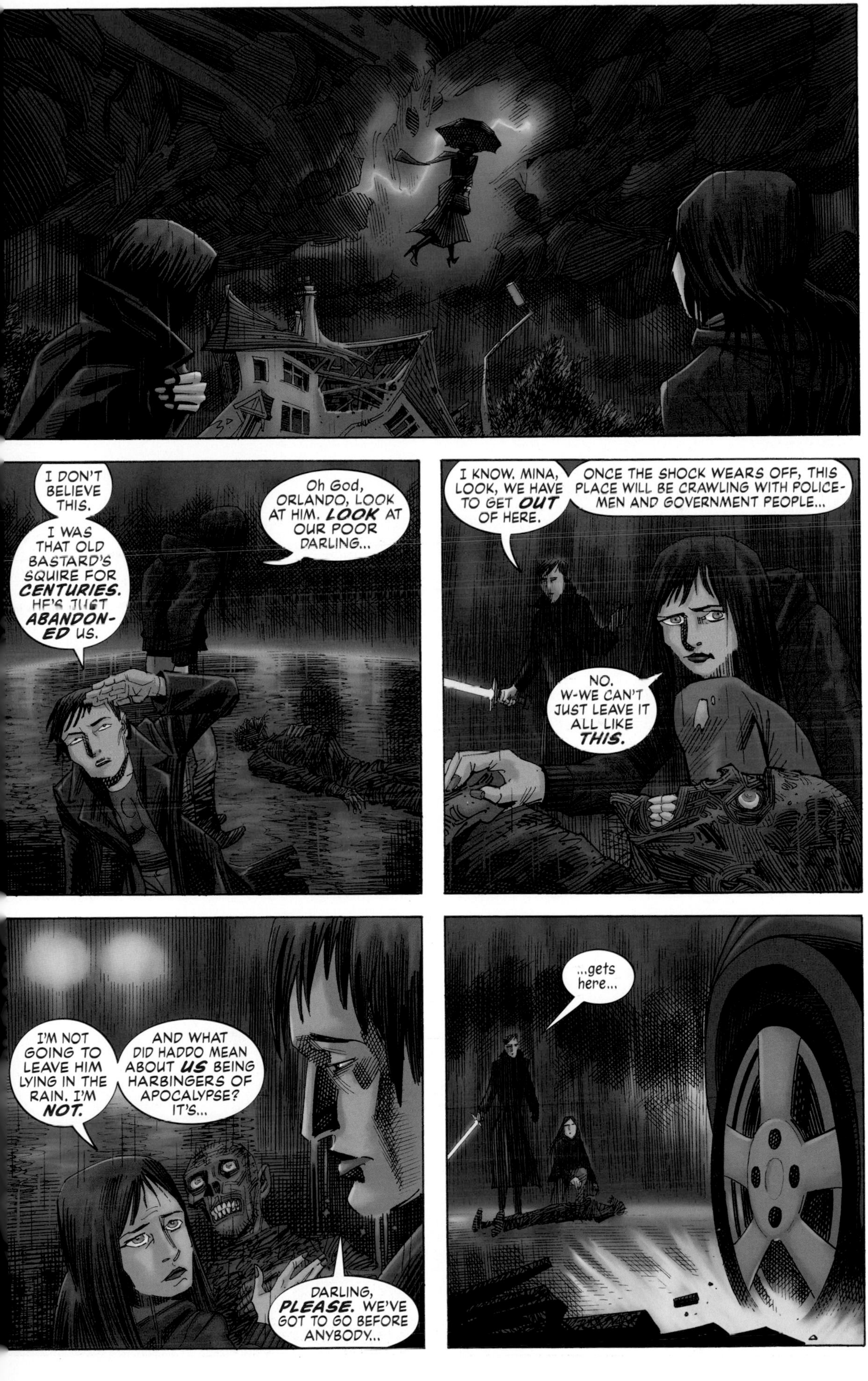
I DON'T BELIEVE THIS.
I WAS THAT OLD BASTARD'S SQUIRE FOR CENTURIES. HE'S JUST ABANDONED US.
Oh God, ORLANDO, LOOK AT HIM. LOOK AT OUR POOR DARLING...
I KNOW. MINA, LOOK, WE HAVE TO GET OUT OF HERE.
ONCE THE SHOCK WEARS OFF, THIS PLACE WILL BE CRAWLING WITH POLICEMEN AND GOVERNMENT PEOPLE...
NO. W-WE CAN'T JUST LEAVE IT ALL LIKE THIS.
I'M NOT GOING TO LEAVE HIM LYING IN THE RAIN. I'M NOT.
AND WHAT DID HADDO MEAN ABOUT US BEING HARBINGERS OF APOCALYPSE? IT'S...
DARLING, PLEASE. WE'VE GOT TO GO BEFORE ANYBODY...
...gets here...

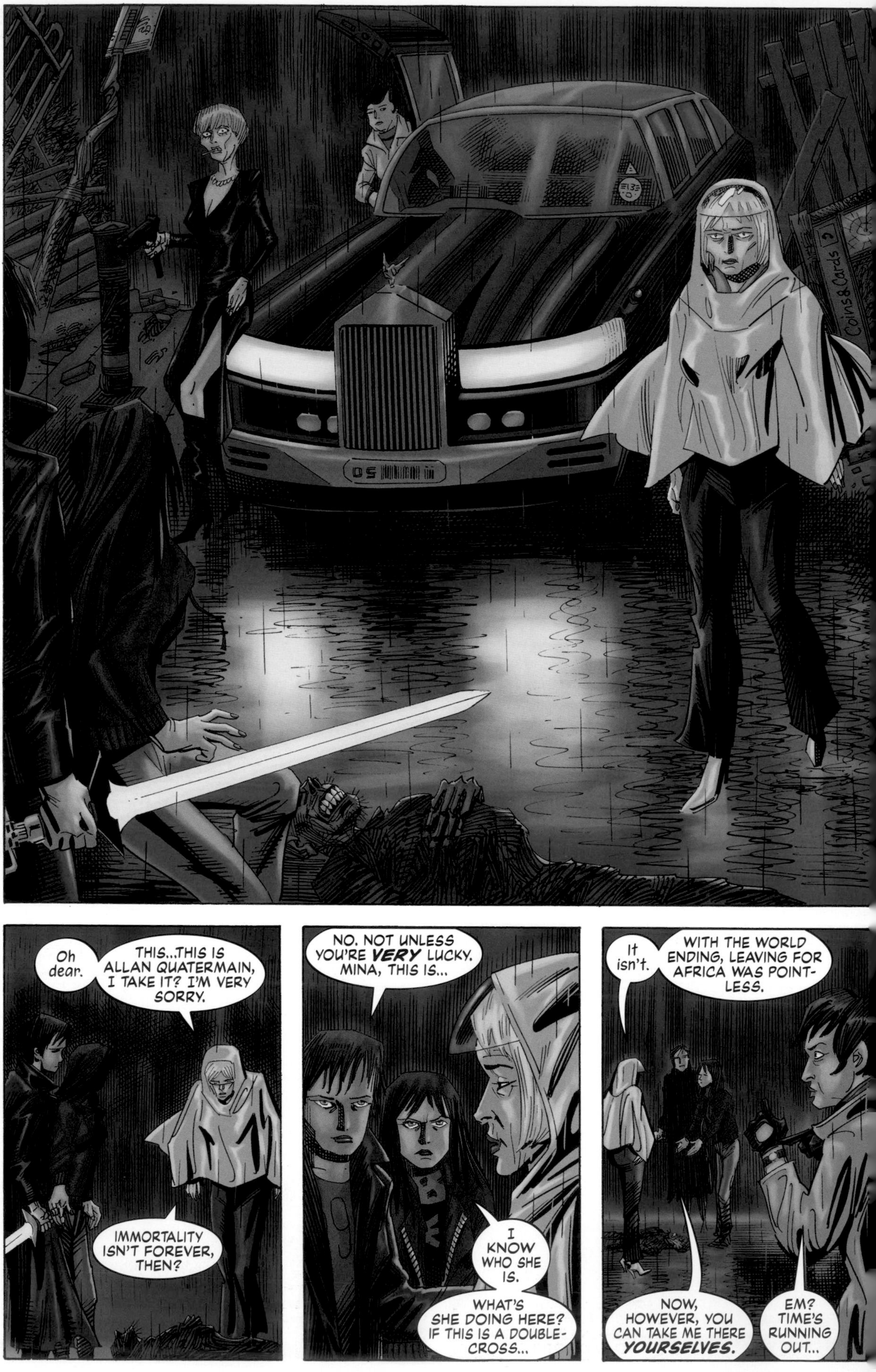
Coins&Cards
Oh dear.
THIS...THIS IS ALLAN QUATERMAIN, I TAKE IT? I'M VERY SORRY.
IMMORTALITY ISN'T FOREVER, THEN?
NO. NOT UNLESS YOU'RE **VERY** LUCKY. MINA, THIS IS...
I KNOW WHO SHE IS.
WHAT'S SHE DOING HERE? IF THIS IS A DOUBLE-CROSS...
It isn't.
WITH THE WORLD ENDING, LEAVING FOR AFRICA WAS POINTLESS.
NOW, HOWEVER, YOU CAN TAKE ME THERE ***YOURSELVES.***
EM? TIME'S RUNNING OUT...

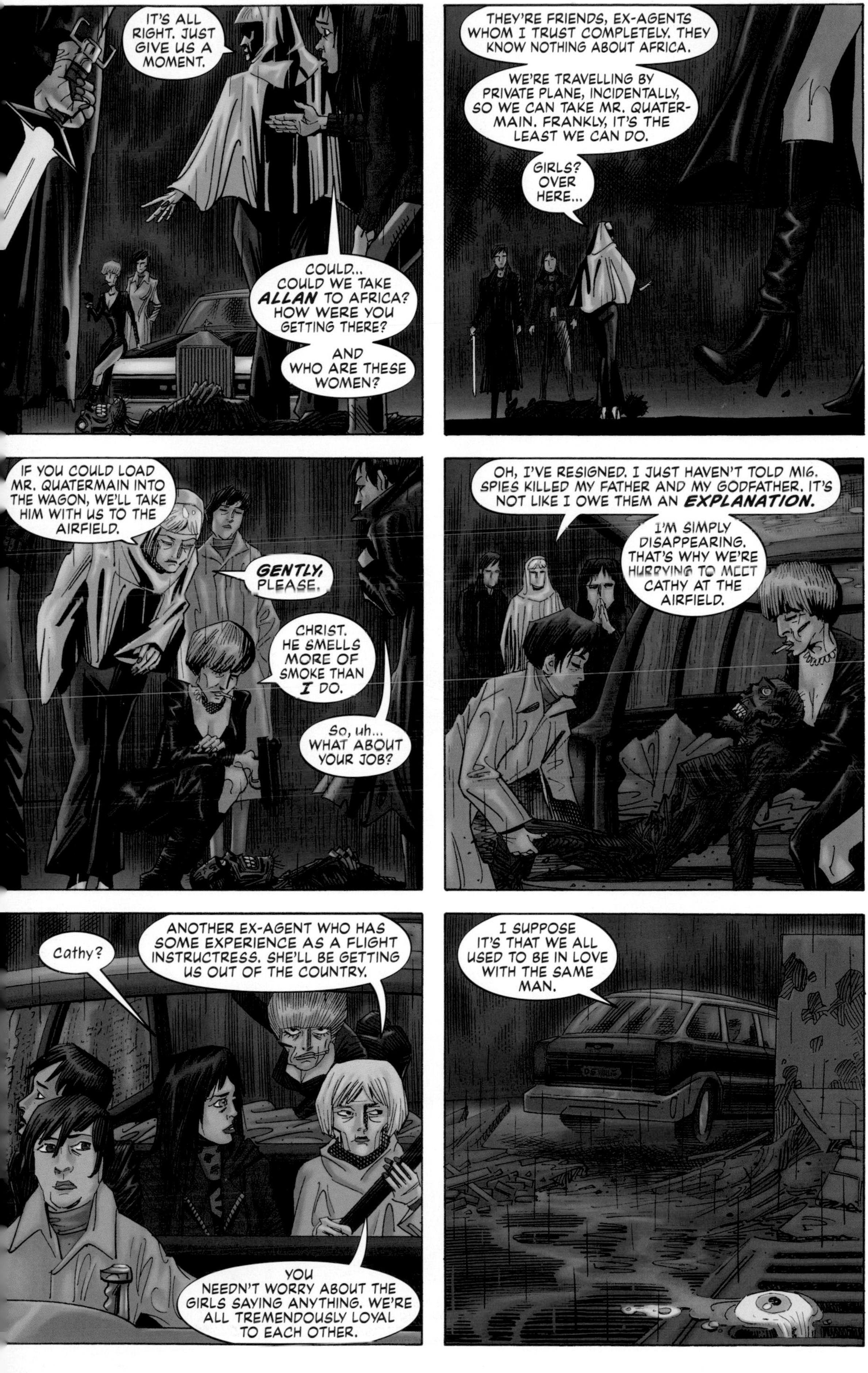
IT'S ALL RIGHT. JUST GIVE US A MOMENT.
COULD... COULD WE TAKE ALLAN TO AFRICA? HOW WERE YOU GETTING THERE?
AND WHO ARE THESE WOMEN?
THEY'RE FRIENDS, EX-AGENTS WHOM I TRUST COMPLETELY. THEY KNOW NOTHING ABOUT AFRICA.
WE'RE TRAVELLING BY PRIVATE PLANE, INCIDENTALLY, SO WE CAN TAKE MR. QUATERMAIN. FRANKLY, IT'S THE LEAST WE CAN DO.
GIRLS? OVER HERE...
IF YOU COULD LOAD MR. QUATERMAIN INTO THE WAGON, WE'LL TAKE HIM WITH US TO THE AIRFIELD.
GENTLY, PLEASE.
CHRIST. HE SMELLS MORE OF SMOKE THAN I DO.
So, uh... WHAT ABOUT YOUR JOB?
OH, I'VE RESIGNED. I JUST HAVEN'T TOLD MI6. SPIES KILLED MY FATHER AND MY GODFATHER. IT'S NOT LIKE I OWE THEM AN EXPLANATION.
I'M SIMPLY DISAPPEARING. THAT'S WHY WE'RE HURRYING TO MEET CATHY AT THE AIRFIELD.
Cathy?
ANOTHER EX-AGENT WHO HAS SOME EXPERIENCE AS A FLIGHT INSTRUCTRESS. SHE'LL BE GETTING US OUT OF THE COUNTRY.
YOU NEEDN'T WORRY ABOUT THE GIRLS SAYING ANYTHING. WE'RE ALL TREMENDOUSLY LOYAL TO EACH OTHER.
I SUPPOSE IT'S THAT WE ALL USED TO BE IN LOVE WITH THE SAME MAN.

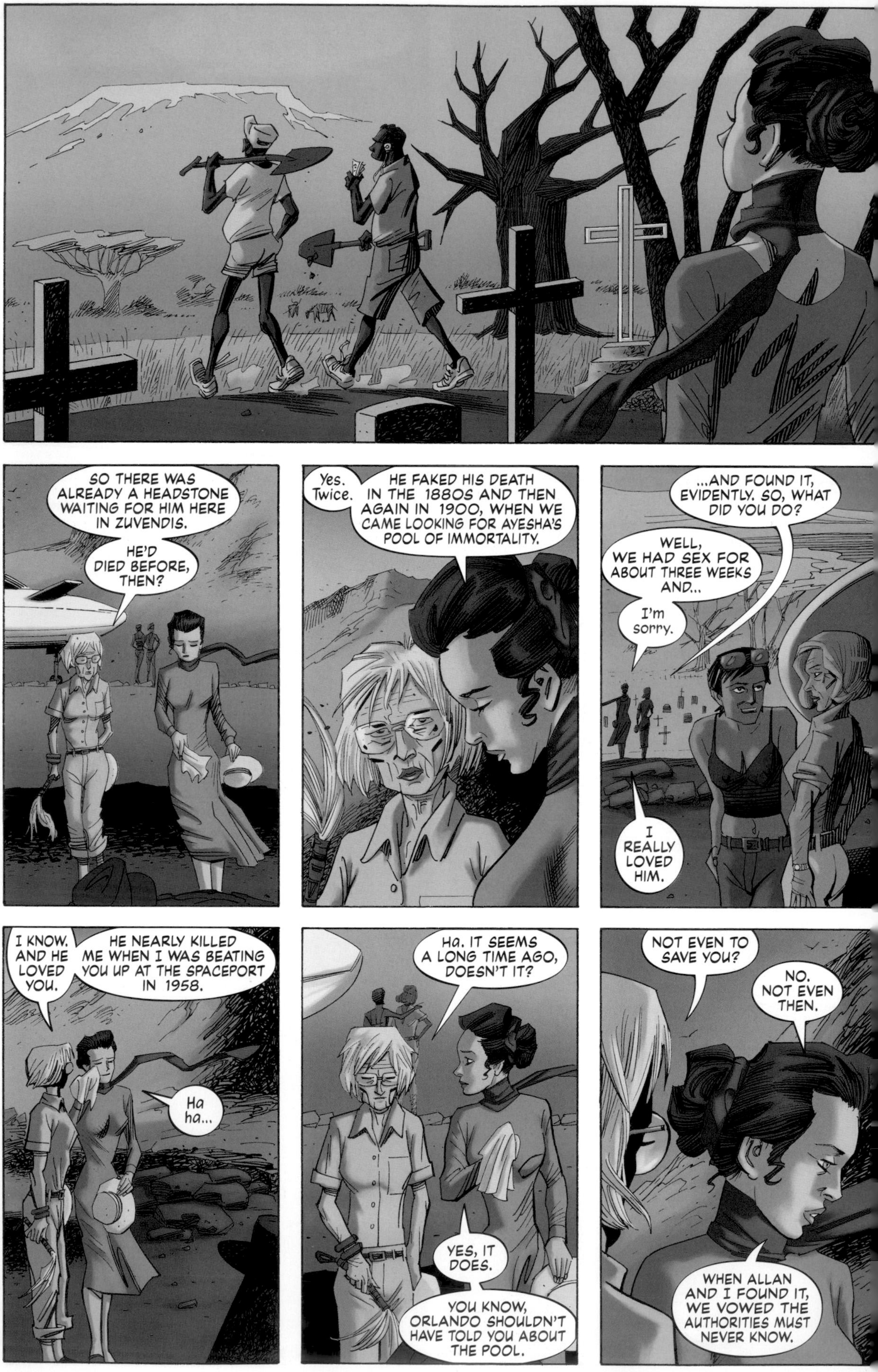
SO THERE WAS ALREADY A HEADSTONE WAITING FOR HIM HERE IN ZUVENDIS.
HE'D DIED BEFORE, THEN?
Yes. Twice.
HE FAKED HIS DEATH IN THE 1880S AND THEN AGAIN IN 1900, WHEN WE CAME LOOKING FOR AYESHA'S POOL OF IMMORTALITY.
...AND FOUND IT, EVIDENTLY. SO, WHAT DID YOU DO?
WELL, WE HAD SEX FOR ABOUT THREE WEEKS AND...
I'm sorry.
I REALLY LOVED HIM.
I KNOW. AND HE LOVED YOU.
HE NEARLY KILLED ME WHEN I WAS BEATING YOU UP AT THE SPACEPORT IN 1958.
Ha ha...
Ha. IT SEEMS A LONG TIME AGO, DOESN'T IT?
YES, IT DOES.
YOU KNOW, ORLANDO SHOULDN'T HAVE TOLD YOU ABOUT THE POOL.
NOT EVEN TO SAVE YOU?
NO. NOT EVEN THEN.
WHEN ALLAN AND I FOUND IT, WE VOWED THE AUTHORITIES MUST NEVER KNOW.

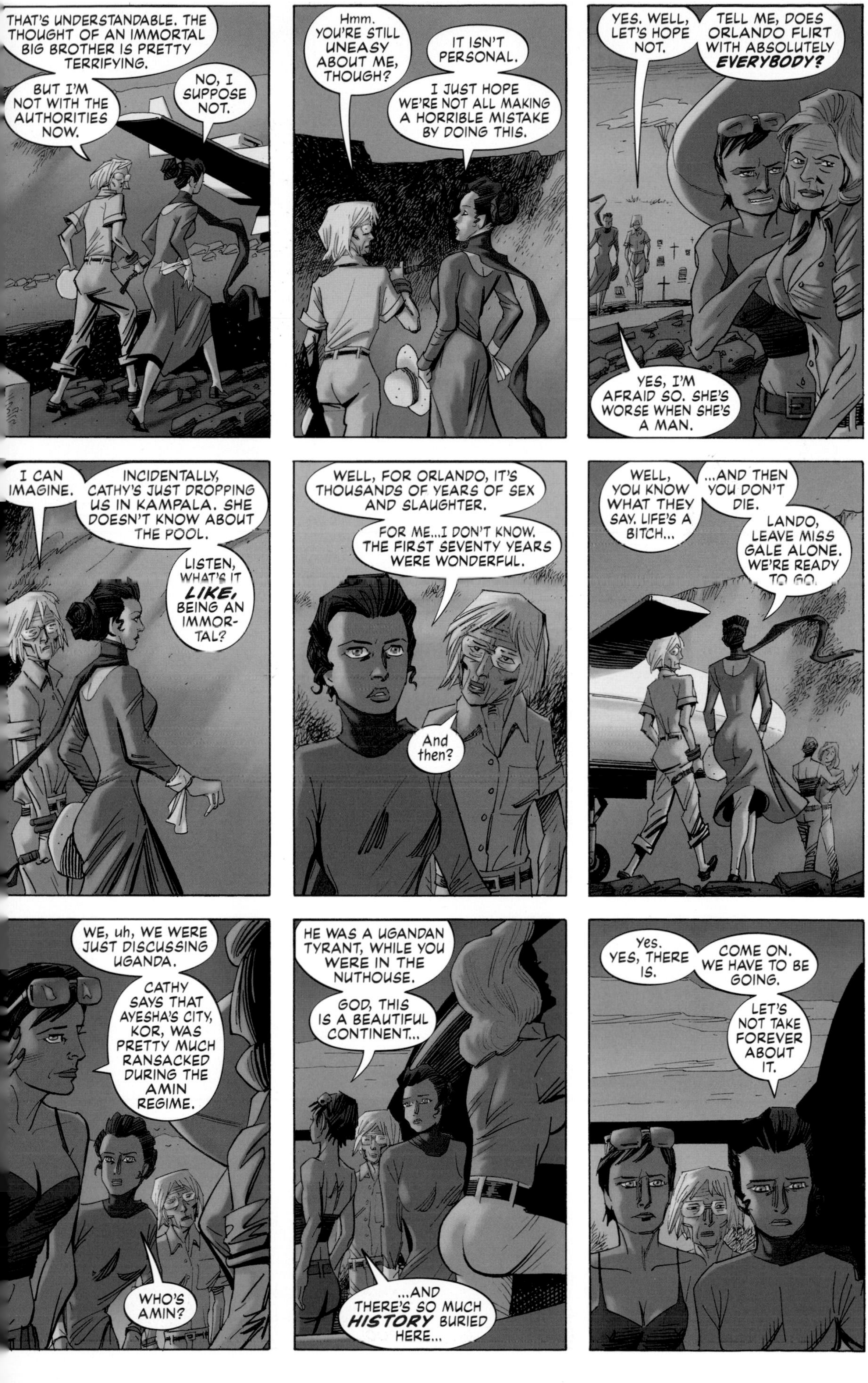
THAT'S UNDERSTANDABLE. THE THOUGHT OF AN IMMORTAL BIG BROTHER IS PRETTY TERRIFYING.
BUT I'M NOT WITH THE AUTHORITIES NOW.
NO, I SUPPOSE NOT.
Hmm. YOU'RE STILL UNEASY ABOUT ME, THOUGH?
IT ISN'T PERSONAL.
I JUST HOPE WE'RE NOT ALL MAKING A HORRIBLE MISTAKE BY DOING THIS.
YES. WELL, LET'S HOPE NOT.
TELL ME, DOES ORLANDO FLIRT WITH ABSOLUTELY EVERYBODY?
YES, I'M AFRAID SO. SHE'S WORSE WHEN SHE'S A MAN.
I CAN IMAGINE.
INCIDENTALLY, CATHY'S JUST DROPPING US IN KAMPALA. SHE DOESN'T KNOW ABOUT THE POOL.
LISTEN, WHAT'S IT LIKE, BEING AN IMMORTAL?
WELL, FOR ORLANDO, IT'S THOUSANDS OF YEARS OF SEX AND SLAUGHTER.
FOR ME...I DON'T KNOW. THE FIRST SEVENTY YEARS WERE WONDERFUL.
And then?
WELL, YOU KNOW WHAT THEY SAY. LIFE'S A BITCH...
...AND THEN YOU DON'T DIE.
LANDO, LEAVE MISS GALE ALONE. WE'RE READY TO GO.
WE, uh, WE WERE JUST DISCUSSING UGANDA.
CATHY SAYS THAT AYESHA'S CITY, KOR, WAS PRETTY MUCH RANSACKED DURING THE AMIN REGIME.
WHO'S AMIN?
HE WAS A UGANDAN TYRANT, WHILE YOU WERE IN THE NUTHOUSE.
GOD, THIS IS A BEAUTIFUL CONTINENT...
...AND THERE'S SO MUCH HISTORY BURIED HERE...
Yes. YES, THERE IS.
COME ON. WE HAVE TO BE GOING.
LET'S NOT TAKE FOREVER ABOUT IT.

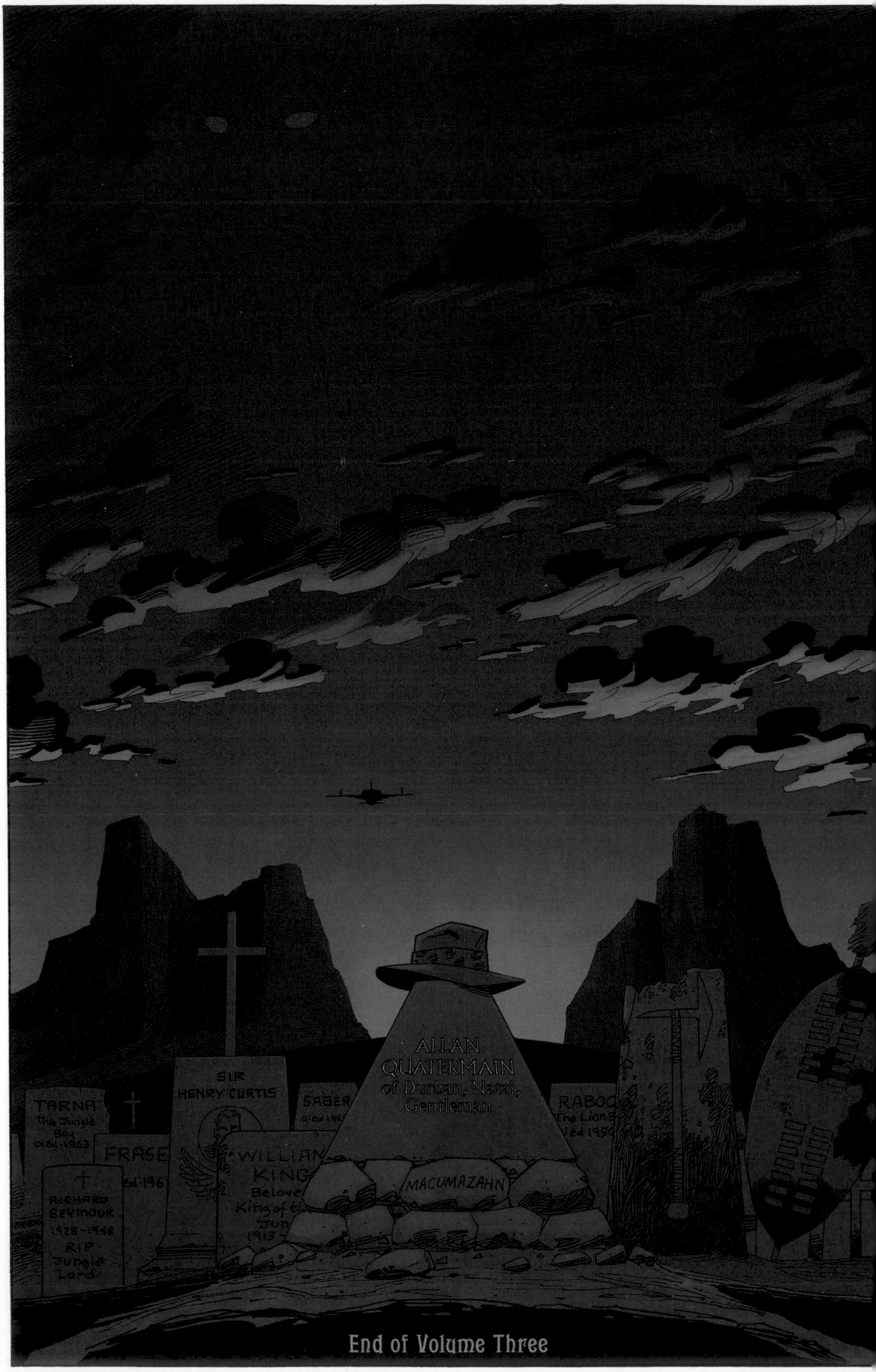
ALLAN QUATERMAIN
of Durban, Natal,
Gentleman
MACUMAZAHN
SIR
HENRY CURTIS
TARNA
The Jungle
Boy
Died 1963
RICHARD
SEYMOUR
1928-1948
RIP
Jungle
Lord
End of Volume Three

MINIONS OF THE MOON
by John Thomas

(Originally serialised in *Lewd Worlds Science Fiction*,
Ed. James Colvin, 183-185, 1969.)

Chapter Three: Saviours

Wheels locked in place, the patient's chair will clearly not be going anywhere. Through an obscuring cumulus of sedatives the notion percolates that these hours are officially allotted to art therapy, the inmates formally encouraged in the reconstruction of their smashed identities from paper, glue and pre-emptively blunted crayons. Listlessly the patient makes pretence at working on a cut-and-paste collage, uselessly adding and subtracting elements simply to foster the appearance of continued work upon a project that in actuality was finished months ago.

If it were thought to be complete there is the danger that it might be taken off by the administrators and exhibited as if the product of a gifted four year-old, with subsequent demands upon the patient to start work on something new. In fact, the thought of more creative toil is actively upsetting. All those hours of careful labour had nothing to do with therapeutic self-expression, but had everything to do with ordinary self preservation.

The assembled picture is the patient's sole escape hatch. It has long been glaringly apparent, even in their fog of pharmaceutics, that they are forgotten by an outside world which they in turn must struggle to remember. There will be no saviour swooping to their rescue, this they are convinced of. No way out, save through the portal they have patiently constructed. Sitting there before the angled drawing board it's possible to let the disinfectant-scented corridors melt into nothingness. It's possible to step, like a true lunatic, into a paper landscape flooded with both memory and meaning.

The immobile wheelchair provides no impediment. The patient walks unfettered in a private realm of dust, and hush, and silver...

Cavor and the Selenites, the moon, 1901: A Cricket-Cap of Thorns

This self was not a self that any sapient biped could have recognised as such. Not predicated on a discrete individual awareness, it was rather the emergent property of an insensate multitude. Lacking for a conceptual equivalent to 'I' or 'We' the nebulous sense of identity had instead coalesced about a core of 'This', a delicately balanced semiotic scent-trace that was not even a word. Almost an entity, this self inhabited a sparse reality comprised of little more than an olfactory map, a pheromonal grid across which the ten thousand chitin-plated engines representing its material corpus acted out their sorties and retrievals. Now, however, the stench-diagram that was its world seemed torn to incoherent fragments as this self attempted desperately to process unfamiliar data; to contain a new and shattering information.

From the point of view of the marooned professor, naturally, the situation was less complex and more readily explained, albeit equally upsetting: having ordered his companions to return to Earth without him in their vessel coated by his marvellous metallic paste, he now faced the inevitable consequences of his selfless sacrifice. As black and lustrous as obsidian, as big as tractors, the unreasoning lunar insects crowded down the narrow rock channel towards him, clambering across their comrades' backs and crushing them to gory splinters in a single-minded rush on their objective. The jet foliage of their antennae twitched and trembled as though in an absent breeze, danced as though to a rhapsody inaudible. Mandibles scissored with a sound like stropping butchers' knives and Selwyn Cavor had the dismal realisation that he'd been backed to the very edge of this particular anomalous patch of the satellite's terrain, which somehow harboured near-terrestrial gravity and atmosphere. One more retreating step would take his spindly-limbed and bulbous body, clad in only jacket, britches, scarf and comically-perched hat into a zone of freezing suffocation that was nonetheless preferable to those advancing jaws, like clashing scimitars. His last breath soured by the now-overwhelming tang of formic acid, he pulled his cap firmly down and then did what he had to.

This self halted in its several dozen tracks. The complicated fragrance-pattern it had been pursuing seemed to suddenly collapse, subsiding to an inert pool of signal which was motionless, the sharpness of the odour fading rapidly on a steep gradient that this self usually associated with an irrevocable and almost instantaneous loss of heat. A knowledge vast and terrible began to crystallise within the net of sensory impressions that were this self's only apprehension of the universe, an ominous assemblage of unprecedented notions that the reeling horde-mind struggled to assimilate.

The swiftly cooling perfume-profile sprawled unmoving at its myriad feet was, this self sensed, a very different and perhaps even a more developed category of self that came from elsewhere. Elsewhere, as defined by this self, was a place beyond its charted atlas of aromas and therefore effectively beyond material existence as that term was understood by the compound intelligence. Further to this, the strange chemical outline of the creature lying still and prone before this self had previously been accompanied by two more scent-shapes of a similar morphology which had by some means since departed past the range of sensory apprehension. Inconceivably, the three intruders had appeared to be autonomous rather than three components of a rival self; a that self. With their evident capacity for somehow organising matter into new forms, such as the containing shell that they'd come here from elsewhere in, it was apparent that these hereto unimaginable non-collective entities were of a higher order of complexity and had arrived here from a consequently higher plane of being. The celestial trinity had left one of their number here, perhaps with the intent of educating and illuminating this self, elevating the perceptions of its colony-awareness to their own exalted altitudes of consciousness. And now this self had driven that redeemer to its death.

A new bouquet began to register in its accustomed fragrance-palette, having notes of awe with undertones of terror and eternity. This self had caught its first whiff of religion.

Mina & the Galley-wag, the Amazon moon-city, 1964: A Harsh Mistress

Mina watched in dismal fascination as the fiery-eyed nude studies that made up the lunar cavalry led out their pale and raucous saurian steeds from a capacious subterranean stable onto the moon's sunlit fields of dust. The fitting of perhaps a thousand ornate silver bridles made a music of deceptive delicacy, starkly punctuated by aggressive reptile shrieks, and the adventuress wondered despairingly how things had reached this sorry state, the very conflict she'd been sent here with the Blazing World's instructions to prevent. The female myrmidons, part of a colony migrated from the universe's rim innumerable aeons since, had lost the male component of their species to a relatively recent plague. Facing extinction without any ready method of fertilisation, they'd resorted to appropriating the remains of stranded lunar pioneer Professor Selwyn Cavor, hoping to extract the late explorer's frozen sperm and thereby propagate their way out of the current crisis. Catastrophically, however, the professor's frosted cadaver had seemingly become an object of religious veneration to the selfsame creatures that had killed him, monstrous insects native to the planetoid and known only as Selenites. These giant arthropods were sure to want their idol back, with the ferocious amazons determined that they shouldn't have it. The forthcoming war, which seemed inevitable now, would put at risk the moon's many terrestrial colonies and force the humans to seek safer habitats in areas of the satellite to which the Blazing World would rather that they did not venture, or at least not yet. Forestalling this eventuality had been her task, at which Mina had proven a conspicuous failure.

Nearby the dark-matter buccaneer whose *Rose of Nowhere* had transported her to this precarious sphere stood with his gawping wooden cabin-girls as keen spectator to the naked army's martial preparations. Dish-sized pupils eagerly drank in every salacious detail of the various straddlings and mountings as the Galley-wag kept up the flimsiest pretence at conversation with one of the women's leaders, a translucently complexioned blonde named Maza. This entirely spurious discourse was effected solely for the purposes of keeping the impatient warrior queen within the baryonic pirate's prurient and appreciative vicinity for as long as was feasible.

'By my endrenching spurt, 'tis as mammariable a fluck of butter-backs as I have hairto wetnessed! Be they mostpartly cumpliable about the slidey-ride, in yer herpinion?'

Such English as Maza had acquired from scattered wireless broadcasts was quite clearly insufficient to the task of fathoming the extra-solar privateer's impenetrable patois. Making the erroneous assumption that her visitor's enquiry must pertain to the bipedal lunar lizards rather than their riders, the imperious moon-queen tossed her white-gold mane dismissively as she replied. Her intonations had a faintly Spanish lilt, no doubt as a result of the stentorian radio transmitter in the Andes previously cited as a source of the unearthly amazons' linguistic expertise.

'The Nak-Kar are a breed somewhere between your own world's dino-saurians and the briefly-reigning giant flightless birds that followed them. Though distantly related to the stubby-winged and brightly-patterned moon-fowl that you have observed amongst our livestock, the Nak-Kar are a much larger and more vicious strain that are ideal as battle-animals. Some think that nothing save their presence keeps at bay the solitary perverted giant who observes all our doings from afar.'

At this the corsair of the starless abyss tipped his barrel-sized head to one side inquisitively.

'I cannaught remagine whyfor anybawdy might engoarge in such a hinterprize.'

Seemingly unfamiliar with the whole idea of disingenuousness, Maza shook her long platinum locks in sympathy with the freebooter's evident incomprehension.

'Nor can I. He was already here when we Lunites first landed many generations since. He keeps to his own lunar neighbourhood, that bluish atmospheric pocket barely visible upon the west horizon. Bald and perhaps four of your Earth metres tall, his only task is seemingly to loiter in an inappropriately skimpy bathrobe, looking on unblinkingly as we perform our daily regimen of military exercises. We refer to him as 'the voyeur'. His is a very different species from our own, or otherwise we would have sought to use his seed in our repopulation strategy. It scarcely need be said that only similar considerations have discouraged us from harvesting your own genetic matter.'

Here the former galley-captive blinked inscrutably and shrugged.

'Waal, let us not dismess my genie-trickle matter so unpheromoniously. I'll grunt yer it's a menstruous inprodability, but I'd pit all me beef and thunder to the attemptation...'

Mina, gazing bleakly at the snapping, squawking ocean of albino dragons and their lance or cutlass-wielding riders, suddenly shook off her trance of lacerating self-recrimination.

'Wait a minute. If you're so convinced that human sperm will do the trick, why haven't you abducted any of the males from the terrestrial moon-bases that are within your reach? From what I know of earthmen they'd most probably consider it a blessing, rather than a violation.'

Maza ventured a small, mournful smile.

'Then they would be aware of us as something other than a wistful myth or a moon-addled fantasy. They would investigate us and then after that, if earthly history is anything to go by, they would subjugate us or destroy us. Better that our tribe fade to extinction for the want of men than suffer such indignities. I fear that your Professor Cavor is our best and only hope, and be assured that we shall fight to the last woman to retain possession of his body. It is true; the native Selenites outnumber us by more than ten to one. Despite superior intellects and greater martial talents we may not survive the coming conflict, but what other option do we have?'

The erstwhile music teacher was still wondering if Selwyn Cavor had ever anticipated that one day women would fight over his body when a perturbation at the corner of her vision captured her attention. The horizon to the south, though icy cold, seemed suddenly to shimmer as if through the curtain of a heat haze. A black, teeming heat haze. Maza too had noticed this phenomenon and called out to her sister-monarch Mysta, mounted at the head of the assembled reptile-riders, in a language that to Mina's ear had vowel-sounds and inflections that were very similar to Cantonese. As Mysta passed on these instructions to the mounted warriors about her, her blonde sibling turned back to their otherworldly guests and with her eyes as sere and unforgiving as an arctic winter offered a translation.

'Be at once to arms. To arms, and to the death. They're coming.'

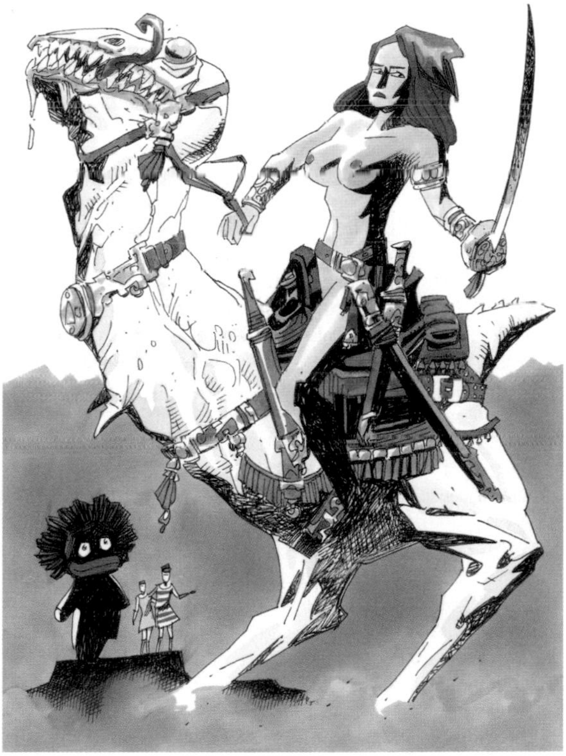

The Baltimore Fun Club, American moon-colony, 1964: Moonbeams, Home in a Jar

The sun's last rays, beguiling as they sloped across the base's largely unused rear equipment hangar, were as colourless and pallid as its first. Taking a deep pull on the smouldering and pungent stick of tea, Pete Munch supposed that was the aspect of his lunar tour of duty that he'd found it hardest to adjust to: no blue skies by day without an atmosphere to scatter solar radiance, and likewise no red at sunset. Nothing except spangled darkness over the horizon, any time of day or night. This monochrome existence, he reflected, must be what it's like to be a character out of a television show. He pictured himself in a sitcom with his straggly hair bobbed and a starched white apron, raising one plucked eyebrow at his screen husband's ineptitude, and was immediately wracked with mirth that noisily propelled the sweet smoke from his flaring nostrils in a series of volcanic bursts. Guilty about the wastage, he held out the reefer in one waving hand for the next man in line to take a hit.

Shaking his head in condescending pity, maintenance crew supervisor Cyrus Pemberton retrieved the spindly offering from between Pete Munch's nicotine-stained fingers, with his languid and yet piercing ivory gaze remaining fixed upon the watery-eyed and coughing senior engineer.

'Hey, Munch, are you sure that you're not a relative of that Norwegian painter guy? That picture of the scream he did is pretty much how I imagine you looked as a baby. No offence.'

While Pemberton took businesslike sips on the sizzling marijuana cigarette, the third of the self-styled Baltimore Fun Club members present in the hangar for the lunar sundown grinned and went on cleaning his high-voltage plasma rifle. Senior charge-hand Marlon Little had the lean build of a dancer and the lethal reputation of a cobra, one of those who had enlisted as a way out of Baltimore's blacker and, inevitably, poorer neighbourhoods. No-one belittled Marlon Little.

'Well, shit. Pemberton, how come a natural New York Times art critic like yourself is up here on the fuckin' moon? You oughtta be back Earthside, bumping up negro intelligence statistics.'

The charge-hand's immediate superior regarded Little with the heavy-lidded and unblinking languor of a hopped-up basilisk, his eyes like yellow warning lanterns through the rising fumes.

'Might I remind you that I'm up here supervising a whole bunch of trigger-happy niggers like yourself? Take two demerits, and I'm docking you a week's pay for the insubordination, plus your general lack of ruliness...' This last touch was too much for even Pemberton. He passed the joint to Little in a mutual barrage of giggles, while Pete Munch attempted to get back in on the conversation.

'Marlon, if you're such a gunslinger, how come you're playing with that sissy plasma rifle?'

Little studied Munch with narrow-eyed disdain while he held down his lungful of the moon-grass. Finally he blew a swirling nebula into the swiftly disappearing sunrays.

'Munch, I thought you pasty motherfuckers just about invented physics? You go lettin' loose with some pump-action number up here on the moon, that scrawny white ass gonna be in orbit.'

The attendant image which this conjured, the bespectacled and hangdog engineer endlessly circling the lunar satellite bearing a smoking shotgun and a look of pained surprise, had all three of them laughing. As the woefully-depleted twist of burning gage returned to him, Pete Munch drew in a scorching breath and gazed contentedly out through the foot-thick screens of flexiglass over a pockmarked reach of taut-stretched shadows and declining light. Membership of the Fun Club, for which he had naturally provided the obscurely witty name, was one of the chief perks of his eighteen-month lunar stint. The hydroponic weed they clandestinely grew up here in the neglected antechambers of *The Pride of Baltimore* was dynamite, and Munch could tell that both his colleagues thought of him as hipper than the average white guy. He was pretty sure they found his frequent monologues on jazz instructive and informative rather than patronising and insufferable for all of their good-natured, ribbing protests to the contrary. He could identify, and figured they appreciated that.

The moon-hemp, though, a hefty mason-jar full of

the stuff, was twice as strong as anything he'd tried in Maryland. He loved the way it made his neurons twinkle in a blissful, shimmering wave and how his every random thought instantly sprouted ornate coral fronds of imagery, especially in an eye-tricking lunar dusk such as the one that now confronted him. He hadn't even known until he got here that the moon had dusks and days and nights. He hadn't realised that it was rotating, with its revolutions timed uncannily so that the same face always looked away from Earth. Twilight transformed the vista to a luminescent ambiguity in which, when suitably intoxicated, anything could be imagined. Now, for instance, with the pot enhancing Munch's visionary capabilities, he conjured a phantasmagoric tableau from the random mottling of shine and shade that stained the distant dunes. Astounded by his own capacity to visualise...maybe he should have been a beatnik artist after all...he pictured an exquisite diorama which even a Coleridge might find difficult to better. Through his mind's eye galloped a delirious and erotic cavalcade of naked women, *Stagman* centrefolds astride fierce alabaster monsters with the waning light become a glinting constellation on their lifted lances, silver helmets and barbaric ornaments. It was a shame, in many ways, that such a fine creative mind as his was being wasted in the engineering corps where there was no-one to appreciate its treasures...

'Munch, I have to ask, are you dead from the hairstyle down by any chance? I mean, you're sitting here just grinning, looking smug. Can't you see all that crazy shit that's going on out there?'

Startled, the neurasthenic ferret of a man spun round to face Cy Pemberton with wild, disoriented eyeballs circling like frantic goldfish in the bowls of his prescription lenses.

'Uh...yes. Yes, I can. Jesus, can you? Fuck!'

Pemberton glared pointedly at Munch in lieu of answer. Marlon Little, shuffling the packing crate he sat on to command a better view of the unscheduled nude revue outside, put down his plasma rifle to give an appreciative whistle at the universe and all of its surprising bounties.

'Huh. You know what's funny? We the only motherfuckers seein' this shit. Everybody else is in the recreation unit watchin' some Montana Wildhack picture what my cousin tells me only got about three titty-shots in the whole thing.'

Having just managed to convince himself that he was looking at some kind of interplanetary incident rather than evidence of his own limitless imagination, Pete Munch was incredulous.

'Gentlemen, we're standing on a scientific threshold of discovery! For God sake, this is man's first glimpse of a whole new civilisation, and you're counting up the boobies? What we've got to do is alert base command, then work out how we're going to accurately write this up...'

Little was laughing openly by now and even the disdainful Pemberton seemed tickled.

'Munch, my man, you have to be aware that your own reputation on the base is, shall we say, hardly a level-headed one. And as for me and Mr. Little here, you may have noticed that we're black. So, say we enter a report about how we saw naked ladies riding big white newts over the moon-hills from this hangar that we're not supposed to be in, let alone be growing dope in, what do you imagine to be the most likely repercussions?' Clearly not expecting a reply, the maintenance chief let his mocking and appraising gaze slide from the speechless engineer back to the Folies Bergère carnage going on beyond the viewport.

'So, no. We ain't writing this one up. Damn. You know what, I wish I had some popcorn.'

And with that the Fun Club settled back to watch the fun.

Mina, the Galley-wag & Maza, *The Rose of Nowhere,* 1964: A Moonlight Flit

'You interfering witch,' snarled Maza. 'Do you even understand what you are doing?'

Clad in Vull's concealing helmet of invisibility and poised behind the furious lunar regent with a similarly unseen 'dagger' (actually a metal slide-rule) pressed against the struggling monarch's windpipe, Mina was beginning to suspect she had disastrously misunderstood the whole delirious situation and therefore elected to keep quiet. Ahead of and below *The Rose of Nowhere* as it slid through the extraterrestrial gloom she could make out the vanguard of the Lunite cavalry, a scything arc of argent weaponry and smooth marmoreal flesh that sliced into the tidal wall of black and gleaming giant ants, approaching from the opposite direction like enraged and scuttling caviar.

As soon as Maza's sister and co-ruler Mysta had charged out of the moon-city with her mounted cohort to engage with the onrushing Selenites, Mina's sequence of actions (far too desperate and impulsive to be called a plan) had simply blossomed into being fully-formed, like Athena from Zeus's brow albeit with little sign of that goddess's wisdom or divine assurance. Switching on her misappropriated helmet at a setting where the light-deflecting headgear was itself not visible, she'd whipped her slide-rule from its pouch and tackled the fair-haired moon-empress from behind, pressing the harmless instrument against her startled captive's throat and hissing threateningly in Maza's ear.

'Now, listen carefully. Nobody else can see or hear me, and the blade that you can feel is razor-sharp. You're going to do exactly as I say, and if you even think of raising an alarm I'm going to slit your gizzard. Nod once if you understand me.'

Maza, even less certain than Mina as to what a gizzard was, had made a tiny inclination of her head, her carmine lips set in a tight and angry line. Compelled thus, the nude beauty had allowed her unseen captor to frog-march her to those vaults beneath the soaring Lunite towers and battlements, accompanied by the Dutch dolls and their anomalous commander who'd all seemed just as bewildered as the lunar potentate herself by this bizarre turn of events. The amazons on guard outside the icy subterranean storage chambers had been ordered by their sovereign to unlock their frigid cellar and then help transport its contents to the Galley-wag's extraordinary sky-boat, never noticing their leader's look of helpless rage or the strained quality her intonations had, much less that she'd left two distinct and separate sets of footprints in the all-pervading lunar dust behind her.

Now, as Mina gazed down anxiously across her captive's shoulder and *The Rose of Nowhere's* starboard rail at the horrific fever-vision of a conflict going on below, she was less sure of her frantically improvised agenda than she'd even been at the scheme's outset. The determined former Mrs. Harker's only certainty was that she must do something to avert this species-threatening disaster, a conviction which a brief glance at the seething battlefield beneath their hovering vehicle served only to entrench: she saw the chestnut-haired Valkyrie Mysta wheel her screaming mount about into a charge, dipping her lance to pierce the thorax of a rearing insectile aggressor and then letting the impaled and squirming behemoth's forward momentum carry it above her head in a slow arc through the slight gravity, to land as pulp and twitching fragments in her wake. Mina watched helplessly as elsewhere in the murderous melee one of the shrieking Nak-Kar lizard-stallions toppled sideways, one leg bitten through by bone-shearing ant mandibles with the result that both the screeching reptile and its luckless fallen rider were at once torn to unrecognisable and gory shreds by the attendant horde of milling Selenites. Swallowing hard, Mina made her attempt to seize the moment.

'Most Resplendent Boson of the Ultimate,' she solemnly intoned, employing a bedizened honorific of the kind she knew that her black-matter comrade favoured. 'We must be about the lowering of our bounty; on stout ropes for preference and to a prudent fifteen feet above the skirmish. Also, would you have some manner of loud-hailing instrument for our reluctant guest to utilise?'

The being previously known as Jackboy Sixty scratched his monstrous head as he considered.

'Waal, there moot be some ferriety o' hullering-trumpet that I can loquate, if yer'll alaw me bit a merement. Minewheel, Peg and Sarey-Jane shall drangle the refrigerbaited cargo to a scrutably frost-rating dipth below our zippelin, as yer surgist.'

The wooden women, with their striped or spangled dresses standing out like stiff flags in some non-existent moon-breeze, set about a winching-down of the rope-cradled object that their captain had instructed them to lower. At the same time their ebon superior emerged from the aft locker with an item which resembled a hand-held trombone augmented by mysterious valves and other, less identifiable components. He held this device up to their angry prisoner and to the faint heat-pattern that his massive extra-human eyes could just make out standing behind the fuming matriarch, tilting his shaggy cranium to one side quizzically, awaiting a response from Mina.

'Give Queen Maza here the megaphone or whatever you call it. Now, your Majesty, you're going to recite the words I whisper to you, and if you can manage that convincingly I promise there's a way that this can be made right without the need for further slaughter. If you cannot manage that, however, then your lifeless body will be flung unceremoniously to that heaving mass of Selenites beneath us. Just do as you're told, and we shall see what happens.'

But what happened was a great surprise to everyone, especially the author of the strategy.

Mysta, Cavor & the Selenites, the moon, 1964: A Sea of Crises

This self halted instantaneously in its multitude of tracks. Somehow suspended in the odourless expanse that hung above the pungent markers and meridians of its awareness-field were the characteristic acid reek and the distinctive sugar-codes which signified the slain redeemer. Visibly, a wave of eerily coordinated motion rippled through its thousands of antennae as these realigned to point in one direction, like black compass-needles swinging inexorably towards a single north.

For Mysta, standing in the stirrups of her blanched and flightless dragon, stained with insect-juice up to

her elbows, the effect was as immediate and as bewildering. The scurrying battalion were, with horrible simultaneity, frozen to perfect immobility save for their feelers that all trembled now towards a point above the carnage and behind her, forcing the moon-warrior to wheel her snarling Nak-Kar steed about so that she too might view the source of the disturbance.

In the glittering black above the battlefield, the strange balloon-boat of their recent visitors was drifting as though upon some aetheric tide, and dangling beneath it was the bluish-grey form of the Lunites' chosen posthumous sperm-donor, headgear frost-fused with his fraying scalp. More startling still from Mysta's point of view was the appearance of her own beloved sister, Maza, standing at the vessel's rail all by herself and calling to the combatants below, aided by some arcane variety of speaking-apparatus. It was to the hypothetical aural distortions of this instrument that Mysta readily attributed the note of strangled tension in her sibling's voice as she addressed the multitude.

'Hear me, my people! Cease your attack. We are returning that which is the totem of our insect neighbours to the place from where we first removed it. We expect them to abandon their hostilities and follow us, and I beseech you not to use this opportunity to injure them. Instead, withdraw to our own fortress and await my imminent return. When we have made full restitution to the Selenites, my friends aboard this craft have promised me that they will next locate a suitable replacement for the seed-source that we have relinquished, and that in a day or so we shall be back amongst you with the promised offering. Mysta, rule wisely in my absence. I'll be with you soon.'

With that the curiously-decorated airboat floated off towards the planetoid's horizon, while the Lunite women's insect adversaries crawled after it en masse, in ordered ranks and at a reverential pace that made it seem as if they were embarked upon some monstrous and inhuman pilgrimage. Obeying Maza's parting wishes, Mysta turned her puzzled cavalry about and led the subdued legion back to the tall spires and pastures of their own encampment, all the while trying to banish from her mind the anxious undercurrent there had been in Maza's clipped inflections and the trapped look in her sister's eyes. She only hoped that their peculiar guests would keep their promise, and that she had not just witnessed the surrender of the only thing which stood between her people and extinction.

Mina and company, the Amazon moon-city, days later: The Sins of the Father

Maza almost pealed with joy as she crushed Minà to her bosom in a hug of gratitude, while the dark-matter corsair and his Dutch dolls looked on jealously. Her platinum hair gleaming in the soft reflected earthlight, the moon-queen expressed her thanks for the ninth time that evening.

'Truly, you and your companions are our saviours. I trust you will forgive the harsh words that we had when I thought you my captor, just before the wisdom of your scheme was made apparent to me. You are neither she-dog nor flat-chested, and I herewith render my apologies. When you returned the frozen corpse of your former acquaintance to the Selenites and then continued on with me aboard in the direction of your native planet, I did not know what to think. But then you showed me the replacement sperm-source that you'd promised, and I understood. My people's prayers were answered, and without potentially annihilating war against the native insect-kind. How can we possibly repay this act of great beneficence?'

The visibly excited Galley-wag was clearly just about to offer his lascivious ideas as to the nature of a suitable reward when Mina thought to intervene. They were all sitting at a banquet table laden down with fresh-cooked moonbirds, shorn of their Easter-egg plumage and then lightly broiled. The centrepiece was one of the black and white spotted metamorphic bipeds that the travellers had earlier seen grazing on the moss-fields just outside the lunar city, crouching roasted on a salver with some form of local fruit stuffed in its mouth. Gesturing to the feast, Mina deflected any thought of further reimbursement, to the obvious annoyance of her lusty pirate colleague.

'Oh, this generous spread is all the thanks we need, your Majesty. With war between the Lunites and the

Selenites averted, the black obelisks which you suggested were responsible for this sphere's intermittent gravity will not be unearthed by terrestrial explorers until such time as my masters wish, thus serving my ends admirably. How is the work with your new donor going, incidentally? I shouldn't mind a last look at him before we embark for our home planet, if that was at all convenient.'

And so it was that soon thereafter Mina found herself in what appeared to be a brightly lit Lunite laboratory somewhere within the city's labyrinthine bowels. Amazon beauties with mask-like expressions busied themselves with pipettes and Petri dishes round the naked cadaver upon its central slab. Their ministrations were already clearly at an advanced stage, and Maza smiled with satisfaction.

'See! We have already managed to extract a myriad of viable spermatozoa and have fertilised a number of donated eggs successfully. Soon, all the moon will be alive with our new benefactor's children. And you say he was a brilliant man; a great professor like our previous donor?'

Mina nodded, studiedly avoiding the accusing glare of her black-matter cohort as he stood beside her, silently berating her for her economy with what he knew to be the truth.

'Yes. The professor was a famous mathematician of tremendous intellect and capability. I can only imagine what a moon-reared generation of his offspring will be like, but, anyway, I'm sure that everything will turn out for the best.'

Voice cracking slightly on the last words of her declaration, caught out in a lie, Mina discovered that her gaze was locked upon the dead stare of the late James Moriarty, dark eyes knowing and sardonic, even in demise. She shuddered inwardly, and wondered what undreamt-of future tribulations she had set in motion here.

What great and monstrous eclipse?

The patient gazes fixedly at their collage, lost in its mesmerising detail. Through an obfuscating ground-fog of incessant medication the idea persists that in these random scraps of glued-together imagery are to be found the scattered fragments of the inmate's past, the shards of their misplaced identity: a minstrel-costumed racial slur clipped from the label on a jar of marmalade; a fine-hatched chapbook illustration that depicts a melodrama villain clinging to a glass ball of unearthly radiance; wooden dolls and naked women and behind it all a full and risen moon, the emblematic flag of lunacy.

So caught up is the patient in their faltering attempt to reconstruct a personality from paste and paper that at first they do not notice the return of the large-breasted doctor, nor the fact that the physician is accompanied by a visitor. This latter party is now crouching by the patient's wheelchair, murmuring in husky female tones that somehow permeate the soporific haze.

'Oh, Mina. Oh, my poor darling. I'm sorry. I'm so sorry.'

Gradually, unhurriedly, the patient's head turns from the patchwork masterpiece to study their first caller in what must be nearly forty years. Outside, through a North London night, the hectic world proceeds towards its end and in the brown blur of an urban firmament no stars are visible, nor over Soho is there any moon.